RENOIR

His Life and Complete Works

SOPHIE MONNERET

In Collaboration With
AGNÈS LIEBAERT

For this present English
language edition:
TODTRI PRODUCTIONS LIMITED,
New York

ISBN: 0-681-10476-7
Printed in Spain by
Fournier Artes Gráficas, S.A.

Editor:

CLOTILDE DE BELLEGARDE

Designer:

LUIS F. BALAGUER

Editorial Assistants:

JOSÉ ANTONIO VÁZQUEZ

PATRICIA NÚÑEZ MILLIERI

ROSA VALLRIBERA I FIUS

ALBERT PUJOL GÁMIZ

English Translation:

RICHARD JACQUES / DISCOBOLE

Design Assistants:

MANUEL DOMINGO PÉREZ

MIGUEL ORTÍZ CATALÀ

Publishing Assistant:

MONSERRAT JUAN PEÑA

Contents

Renoir.

The most Parisian of the Impressionists, Pierre-Auguste Renoir was born in Limoges in 1841. His father was a tailor and his mother a dressmaker. In 1844 or early in 1845 his parents left the city of porcelain and went to live in the Louvre district of Paris, – first in the Rue de la Bibliothèque, where their seventh son Edmond was born, and from 1855 to 1868, in the Rue d'Argenteuil. Renoir had a gift for music. When he sang in the Saint-Eustache choir, his teacher Charles Gounod, the composer of *Faust* (1859), predicted that he would become an opera singer. But his inclination towards drawing won the day. And since in the Renoir family it was considered, in best Limoges style, that the future of a painter and decorator was guaranteed, that was the career Auguste embarked on.

From the age of thirteen, Renoir went to work like his brothers – Henri a goldsmith's engraver, and Victor a tailor. He entered as apprentice to a painter on porcelain and spent four years there. He learnt to decorate plates, cups, and lamps and came to be called "little Rubens" by his workmates, who were dazzled by his skills. When the business went bankrupt, young Auguste turned his hand to different jobs – painting blinds, fans, and even a composition for a Paris café.

The Empress Eugénie had made the 18th century fashionable and Auguste Renoir drew his inspiration from the French painters Watteau, Lancret, and Boucher, of whom he said: "*Diana Bathing* was the first painting to have thrilled me and I loved it for the rest of my life in the way you love your first loves." From that period the artist would keep a lively interest in craftwork and decoration, which he would always practice with pleasure, working to order. In 1861 Émile Laporte, whom he met at the evening classes of the École de Dessin et de Décoration in the Rue des Petits-Carreaux, took him to enroll at the studio of a highly appreciated master, Charles Gleyre, where Whistler had also studied for a time. He would be more marked by the friendships he made among his fellow pupils than by the rather classical instruction of his teacher, but he would never forget his advice: "Choose very young models, decrepitude sets in at eighteen." And it was his teacher who awakened in him his desire to create a paradise on his canvases.

He was admitted to the École des Beaux-Arts in 1862 and worked frequently at the Louvre, where he made the acquaintance of a friend of Manet, Fantin-Latour. His kindness, modesty, and talent brought Renoir sincere friends and useful protectors. At Gleyre's he met Monet, Sisley, and Bazille, three young men who had nothing but scorn for official painting. Their idols were Delacroix or Manet, the same Manet who had just caused a scandal at the Salon des Refusés (1863) by exhibiting *The Bath*, known as *Le Déjeuner sur l'herbe* (The Picnic). On fine days the four companions went with knapsacks on their backs to paint "from life" in the forest of Fontainebleau, the "open-air studio"

Fantin-Latour's painting The Studio in Batignolles *(Musée d'Orsay, Paris) is a tribute to Manet, represented in front of his easel and surrounded by his friends, painters (Renoir in the hat, Monet, and Bazille) and writers (Zola, Astruc, Maître, and Schölderer).*

Manet kept this photograph of the young Renoir, taken by A. Lefèvre, in his album. The friendship between the two painters went back to the days when they haunted the Café Guerbois.

of all European landscape painters. As they worked in the woods, they had some fruitful encounters: not only Virgile Narcisse Diaz, who advised Renoir to give prominence to the light tones and always to work with a model, but also Camille Corot and Gustave Courbet, the master of the Realist generation. From him Renoir learnt to use the painting knife and a thicker paste.

In 1864 Gleyre closed his studio, "to the great regret of his pupils," as Bazille wrote. It was at that time that Renoir became involved with the Le Cœur brothers; Jules, the painter, who took him to Marlotte, and Charles the architect. They were the friends and benefactors of his early days. He was also captivated by one of his first models, Lise Tréhot, who became his mistress. *Le Cabaret de la Mère Antony, La Bohémienne, Lise with Sunshade, The Pont des Arts* were done during those formative years which bring together the influence of Corot's landscapes, Courbet's realism, and Manet's modernity.

Renoir stayed for a time with Sisley and then with Bazille, first in Rue Visconti in Saint-Germain-des-Prés in 1867, and then, 1868, Rue La Condamine in the Batignolles district, just two steps from the Café Guerbois. The spot had been launched by Manet and had become a meeting place for the new school, known at the time as the "Batignolles group." Its pillars? Artists like Constantin Guys, Fantin-Latour, Degas, Cézanne, Monet, Bazille; writers like Duranty, Zola, Théodore Duret (a cognac merchant and the first historian of Impressionism), Mallarmé, Villiers de l'Isle-Adam; the photographer Nadar, the engraver Félix Bracquemond, and the erudite and dilettante Edmond Maître. Amidst the fumes of wine and tobacco, diatribes and laughter, the great pictorial revolution of the turn of the century was plotted.

It was on the banks of the Seine in 1869, at "La Grenouillère", a bathing establishment and pleasure garden, that Impressionism was really born. Renoir was taken to the fashionable spot by Prince Bibesco, for whom he was doing decoration work at the time. The painter often visited his parents, who had retired to Louveciennes in 1868. He then joined Monet in that "Trouville on the banks of the Seine" where they set up their easels side by side. All the fundamental elements of Impressionism were already present in their different versions of *La Grenouillère*: the play of shadow and light, comma-shaped brush strokes, sketchy figures.

A difficult period for Renoir, who complained at the time that he did not have enough money to buy paints, and for Monet, whose family had just cut off his allowance. Unlike his colleagues Cézanne, Bazille, Sisley, and even Monet, Renoir lived exclusively by his brush. "I am at Monet's practically every day where, by the way, we are growing old... We do not eat every day, but I am still happy because, for painting, Monet is good company," he wrote to Bazille.

Later he was to confide: "I would have thrown in the towel on more than one occasion if my old Monet had not given me a hand up." The confession of a man who, throughout his life, would be surrounded by friends ready to give him encouragement at times when he was seized by doubt and even went so far as to destroy his works. And yet, depressive as he was, he had only one desire: to bring joy to his canvases. "For me, a picture must be a likeable thing, joyful and pretty, yes, pretty! There are enough unpleasant things in life without us making more."

Renoir had long shared the obsession of all painters: to be admitted to the Salon. Accepted in 1864 and 1865 with a portrait of his friend Sisley's father in the second year, he was turned down in 1866 and 1867, upon which he signed a petition with Bazille demanding a new Salon des Refusés. In 1868, *Lise with Sunshade*, a white figure in the open air, was accepted. Although it was badly placed, the painting, which is somewhat reminiscent of Courbet, marked the beginning of his fame, as it drew the attention of critics and caricaturists.

The following year came the great aesthetic break constituted by his canvases of *La Grenouillère*. However, his contribution to the Salon was a well-behaved one, *In Summer*. To the Salon of 1870, he sent *Bather* and *Woman of Algiers,* a prudent sacrifice to the taste of the jury: the former is academic and the latter orientalist. He himself appears, along with Bazille and Monet, in Fantin-Latour's painting *A Studio in Batignolles*, a tribute to Manet surrounded by his admirers and a sort of birth rite of the new school.

In 1870 in The Artist's Studio, Rue La Condamine *(Musée d'Orsay, Paris), Bazille represented the regulars who had been visiting him since 1868. Bazille, in the centre being painted by Manet, is showing one of his canvases to Manet or, according to other people, to Monet, or to Zola, in yet another version. Sisley is sitting on the table and Renoir is watching the scene from the stairs.*

IMPRESSIONISM AND THE JOY OF LIVING

When the war of 1870 broke out, Renoir was recruited for a regiment of chasseurs. He did not fight in the battles owing to an attack of dysentery, but he was deeply affected by the death of Bazille, killed at the age of twenty-nine. During the Commune, the painter who "wanders penniless from Paris to Versailles and from Versailles to Paris" had friends in both camps. He had no taste for politics and his commitment throughout his life can be summed up in what he called "the politics of the cork": drifting along on the tide of events. From 1871 to 1873, Renoir rented a studio in Rue Notre-Dame-des-Champs, one of the most popular streets with artists. That was the time of his encounters with Verlaine, whom he already knew, and with Rimbaud at the houses of Edmond Maître and the musician Cabaner, rediscovered today by Colomer. It was also the time of the purchase by Durand-Ruel of his *Pont des Arts*, the beginning of a constant, faithful relationship with the art dealer who defended Impressionism so skillfully.

The Salon of 1872 rejected his *Parisiennes en Algériennes*, which is a sensitive reflection of the influence of Delacroix. It was the last canvas that Lise posed for; she went out of his life to marry an architect. Shortly afterwards the artist embarked on an extremely ambitious work, *Bridle Path in the Bois de Boulogne*, for which he obtained authorization to work in the banqueting room of the Military School. In a style which is still close to Courbet, it depicts Madame Darras and the young son of Charles Le Cœur. Also turned down by the jury in 1873, the painting was hung in the Salon des Refusés, organized under the chairmanship of Harpignies.

That year Renoir rented an apartment at 35 Rue Saint-Georges. He remained in the building until 1884; his younger brother, the journalist Edmond Renoir also lived there. He was to be an ardent advocate of his art. Monet, who had taken refuge with his wife and son in England, returned and settled at Argenteuil where Renoir visited him frequently. They worked together but each one stuck to his preferences: Monet never tired of landscapes, Renoir engaged in a passionate scrutiny of female faces and forms. Their styles, however, were sometimes so similar that in 1913 they found it hard to tell which of them had done a *Pool with Ducks* around 1873.

The beautiful Camille posed tirelessly for one or the other. For Manet too, who joined them for the summer of 1874. The new manner inaugurated at "La Grenouillère" triumphed with its colors contrasted

N'a eu qu'une année pour se préparer, et se trouvant un peu en retard.　　　　C'était bien la peine de tant se presser.

according to Chevreul's theories, its allusive forms, its small rapid brush strokes which blend the figures with nature. The sailboats on the Seine alternate with views of gardens and young women crossing meadows of flowers. Argenteuil and Louveciennes were the setting for that apotheosis of light and, briefly, Fontenay-aux-Roses, where Charles Le Cœur had just bought a house. But in late 1873 or early 1874 there was a definitive estrangement from the Le Cœur family over a love letter addressed by Renoir to Charles' daughter, a girl of sixteen. After the disappointment of the Salon of 1873, the project for a group exhibition, which had been mooted years before, took shape and some of the preparatory meetings were held at Rue Saint-Georges.

Where to hold the exhibition? The generous Nadar, described by Théodore de Banville as a "giant intoxicated with joy and crowned with a living flame," lent his abandoned premises in the Boulevard des Capucines. Edmond Renoir undertook to draft and print the catalogue

This engraving from 1873 shows a scene at La Grenouillère, a pleasure garden aboard a boat with gangways moored on the banks of the Seine. The spot was a favourite haunt of people in search of amusement in the eighteen-seventies.

Chacun, soyez-en sûr, trouvera à faire son petit feuilleton.

Les critiques dans l'exercice de leurs fonctions.

Humorous drawing by Cham (Amédée Noé) alluding to the Salon of 1869.
The painters who wanted to exhibit at the official Salon which opened its doors in Paris once a year had to present their works to a jury beforehand. If the jury rejected a picture, they wrote an "R" on the back.
In 1869, Renoir's painting In Summer, in which he painted his friend Lise, was accepted and hung at the Salon.

of that cooperative limited company of painters, sculptors, and engravers. The exhibition opened on 15 April 1874. Among the thirty painters who hung their works there many were destined for glory: Boudin, the engraver Bracquemond, Cézanne, Degas, Monet, Berthe Morisot, Pissarro, Renoir, Sisley. The only ones missing were Fantin-Latour and Manet, who remained faithful to the Salon. They were all aware that they had reached a crucial moment in their careers.

Among the canvases on show was *Impression, Sunrise* by Monet. "What does the canvas represent? You will see, in the leaflet, *Impression, Sunrise*. An impression I was sure; I also said to myself, there must be something impressive in it," wrote Louis Leroy in *Le Charivari*, the famous satirical broadsheet. And so Impressionism was baptized.

Six paintings and a pastel by Renoir (*Dancer, The Box at the Theatre, Reapers, The Parisienne, Flowers, Woman's Head* and a sketch) show the mastery and versatility of his talent. *The Box at the Theatre* received several favorable notices, among them the one by Marc de Montifaud, the pseudonym of a friend of Villiers de l'Isle-Adam. 3,500 visitors guaranteed the success of the exhibition, but the same number of francs from the sale of paintings was not enough to cover the expenses. In December Renoir, Bureau, and Sisley were given the task of winding up the company.

If that event was a milestone in the history of art, it was a moral and financial disappointment for Renoir at the time: "The only thing we took away from the exhibition is the label Impressionist, which I loathe," he declared.

His group had managed to hold their first exhibition, but they were no better thought of for that. On the contrary, their works were the target of lampoonists and caricaturists, the most hackneyed joke being: "The works can be looked at just as well upside down as the right way up."

In 1875, Renoir cajoled Monet, Sisley, and Berthe Morisot into attempting a public sale with him, to which he sent nineteen canvases. The atmosphere between the adversaries and partisans of Impressionism was very stormy. The police even had to be called in to calm down the students from the Beaux-Arts who had come to demonstrate against that "scandalous painting." Paul Mantz, in *Le Temps*, voiced the general opinion: "We should take no notice of these chimerical spirits who imagine that we take their slovenliness for candor."

The sale was nevertheless the beginning of success for Renoir. The painter from Lausanne, Auguste de Molins, who had taken part in the exhibition of 1874, bought *Young Woman in the Fields* and Victor Chocquet, who had been present at the memorable set-to, came on the second morning to commission a portrait from Renoir. As for the publisher Charpentier and his wife, who had bought *Fisherman* and *Garden with Dahlias*, they would soon provide Renoir with the support of all their financial, intellectual, and worldly power.

The second Impressionist exhibition was held in 1876 at Durand-Ruel's, number 11 Rue Le Peletier. It was a disaster thanks to the murderous article by the highly influential Albert Wolff in *Le Figaro*. However it affected Renoir less than others, as most of his canvases belonged to his new enthusiasts, Chocquet and Dollfus. A portrait of Delphine, the daughter of the merchant Legrand, attracted attention to his remarkable skills as a child portraitist.

G. C. A., Paris   794 Montmartre. — La rue Pigalle — Nouvelle Athènes.

That year he discovered Rue Cortot, on the Butte Montmartre, a studio surrounded by an immense garden in the grounds of an old folly, the site of the present Musée du Vieux-Montmartre. That allowed him to paint the huge decorative figures commissioned by the Charpentiers for the staircase of their private mansion in Rue de Grenelle. It also allowed him to paint the large pictures in the open air that he had always dreamed of.

The period 1874-1884 was his golden age. *The Square de la Trinité*, *The Seine at Champrosay*, the village where Delacroix had been laid to rest and where Nadar and the Daudet had their summer residences, *Les Grands Boulevards*, *The Garden at the Rue Cortot*, *The Swing,* all his pictures, landscapes or genre scenes express the happiness of painting. It was a carefree time; Renoir had a crowd of younger friends, of whom some were painters: Franc-Lamy, Goeneutte and Michel de L'Hay, who has been rediscovered today by the work of Michael Pakenham. Others were civil servants, such as Georges Rivière and Eugène Lestringuez, or worked for Havas, like Paul Lhote. They went dancing with models, budding actresses, or girl workers from Montmartre at the "Moulin de la Galette". The Guerbois era was at an end. Now they met at "La Nouvelle Athènes" in the Place Pigalle, a café where artists rubbed shoulders with poets next to the models' hangout. His sentimental liaison with an actress, Madame Henriot, who appears in *Lady in Blue* and several other canvases, brought Renoir into close contact with the world of the theatre. But he was also welcomed in other circles; he was a regular attender at Théodore de Banville's Thursdays, Daudet's dinners, and the monthly Wednesdays of Eugène Meunier, known as Murer. Guillaumin introduced his friends to this unusual character. A restorer in the Boulevard Voltaire, writer and collector of Impressionist paintings, he and his sister received guests

At the Nouvelle-Athènes café, painters and writers got together with Manet and Degas to talk about the future of painting. At those gatherings, Renoir met Caillebotte, a lover of the new painting, who bought canvases from the Impressionists.

Dance at the Moulin de la Galette in Montmartre. In his memoirs (1921) Georges Rivière says that on Sundays Lamy, Goeneutte, Renoir and he used to go there. Workers went to dance there and the painter found models who were different from the ones who used to pose in the artists' studios.

behind his workshop and recommended his painter friends to his customers. He acquired the *Parisiennes en Algériennes* after it had been turned down by the Salon, and eventually owned thirty Renoirs.

Renoir also accompanied Franc-Lamy to Nina de Callias's soirées; she was the generous princess of the Bohemian world and Charles Cros and Villiers de l'Isle-Adam were her regular dinner guests, along with the young actress Jeanne Samary and the beautiful composer Augusta Holmés. A host of musicians and music lovers now belonged to Renoir's entourage; since 1861 he had taken up the cudgels on behalf of Wagner, a composer who was in high favor with the Batignolles group. He shared his passion for music with Bazille, Edmond Maître and Cabaner, whom he still saw frequently. The composer Emmanuel Chabrier was another habitué of the Rue Saint-Georges and in 1883 played *España* with such passion that the strollers clustered under the windows shouting "Olé!"

At the third exhibition organized by the Impressionists (1877), Renoir sent twenty-one canvases, among them the portraits of *Madame Charpentier, Madame Alphonse Daudet,* and of the member of parliament Spuller. *Dance at the Moulin de la Galette* was the highlight, along with *The Swing* lent by Caillebotte. Shortly afterwards, with a second public sale, fifteen of his canvases and a pastel sold for a total of 2,005 francs.

While the exhibition was on, his friend Rivière, on his advice, published four numbers of a magazine entitled *L'Impressionniste,* in which Renoir himself explained his ideas, signing the article "a painter."

Life was still difficult and the artist had even asked Gambetta, whom he met at the house of the collector Cernuschi, whether there was any chance of his being appointed curator of a provincial museum. The project came to nothing and Renoir tried his luck at the Salon once again; in 1878 he sent *Le Café.* It was the Charpentiers who urged him to take the step. Georges Charpentier, "the angels' publisher and the angel of publishers," as he was nicknamed by Flaubert, published the Naturalists (Zola, Flaubert, Alexis, Maupassant). His wife had a salon where she welcomed novelists, Impressionists, actors (Coquelin,

Jeanne Samary) and singers (Bruant and Yvette Guilbert, so highly thought of by Toulouse-Lautrec). There also were to be found the "upper crust" of the aristocracy (the duchesses of Uzès and Rohan) and politics (Clémenceau, Jules Ferry, Gambetta). There was no formality about those evenings, where everyone had as much fun as serious discussion.

Monet, Sisley, and Renoir often had recourse to the generosity of their hosts at difficult times. Paraphrasing an expression in vogue at the court of Louis XIV, Renoir introduced himself to Madame Charpentier as "the most devoted of ordinary painters." For her he did menus, decorations, frames for mirrors, and several portraits. At the Salon of 1879, the one entitled *Madame Charpentier and Her Children* was a resounding success.

To support Naturalism in painting, Georges Charpentier now launched a magazine, *La Vie moderne*, accompanied by exhibitions. The one in June was devoted to Auguste Renoir's pastels.

In spite of the reticence which Impressionism still aroused, his reputation was confirmed and the delicacy of his children's portraits brought in commissions. New enthusiasts appeared. The Russian banker and collector, Charles Ephrussi, director of the *Gazette des Beaux-Arts*, introduced him to the Cahens d'Anvers. Charles Deudon, the owner of the shop "Old England" and an ardent lover of Japanese prints, recommended him to the old diplomat Paul Bérard who, in turn, introduced the painter to his friends the Grimprels. The under-secretary of state for the Fine Arts, Turquet, commissioned him to paint a portrait of his wife and daughter in 1880. Doctor Paulin spoke in his favor to Senator Goujon, who asked him to do portraits of his four children.

The Pont des Arts in Paris. Renoir, who was deeply influenced by photography, immortalized several urban scenes in an attempt to capture the snapshot effect of instantaneousness.

From 1879, Renoir often stayed with the Bérards at the Château de Wargemont near Dieppe. He painted the members of the family and decorated the villas in the surroundings, among them that of Doctor Blanche, the famous alienist, father of the young painter Jacques-Émile Blanche, a friend of Edmond Maître. His great composition *Mussel Fishers at Berneval* shows a concern for local color which was a concession to the taste of the Salon. It appeared there, as did *Young Girl Sleeping* with its underlying eroticism. Cézanne persuaded Zola to write an article in *Le Voltaire* supporting the works of Renoir and Monet, whose works had been badly placed by the hanging committee. When he decided to return to the Salon, Cézanne, Sisley, and Monet did the same, causing serious dissention among the Impressionist group, which forbade its members to take part in both their shows and those of the state. The following year he wrote to Durand-Ruel to explain his refusal to join his former colleagues at the group exhibition that he was preparing: "How are we to become known when there are hardly fifteen art-lovers in the whole of Paris capable of liking a painting if it is not in the Salon, while there are eighty thousand who would not even buy a nose if the painting has not been hung in the Salon. That is why I send two portraits every year, however little that may be." The letter was posted in Algeria. Indeed, since the commissions for portraits had begun to flow in, Renoir could afford to travel. He had gone to join his brother in the South and, accompanied by Lestringuez, Lhote, and Cordey, had decided to cross the Mediterranean and discover North Africa, which had been the dream of all the Romantic artists.

The country was a disappointment. It rained, he could not find models. "The women so far are unapproachable," he complained. His pictures

reflect his dissatisfaction and are lacking in the grace which had always infused them previously. On his return, Renoir had arranged to meet Duret in London, but work on *The Luncheon of the Boating Party* kept him in Chatou. It was Whistler, who had come to lunch at Fournaise' house, who undertook to tell Duret that the journey had been cancelled. The change of plan was not a mere whim. Renoir was now approaching forty and awaiting the arrival of a young dressmaker from Champagne who was coming to pose for him: Aline Charigot, who came from Essoyes, in the Aube, and turned his life upside down. Enchanted by "the cat in her" – his own words – he would never leave her again. He married her in 1890. Her portrait, painted around 1885, shows a dazzling young woman in a harmony of yellows and blues.

THE ANXIETIES OF THE INGRES PERIOD

New loves and new art-lovers acted on his very conception of art: "I have suddenly become a traveller and have been seized by a fever to see the Raphaels," he announced to Madame Char-

Degas took this photograph of Renoir with Mallarmé in 1895 at the Manets' house, where Berthe Morisot entertained her friends. Renoir had been a regular visitor since 1887.

pentier in October 1881. The painter visited Venice, Rome, Naples, Capri, and even made the leap across to Sicily to sketch a portrait of Wagner at the request of some musical friends. The composer, who was finishing *Parsifal*, gave him just thirty-five minutes of pose.

Two quite different paintings reveal his aesthetic concerns: *Venice, Fog*, with its essentially Impressionistic mists, and *Blonde Bather*, painted on Capri, where the model was Aline, whom he had discreetly taken along with him. That work, with its cleanly drawn contours, set the tone for the period to come. We feel the influence of the Raphaels in the Farnese and the frescoes in Pompeii, but also that of Ingres, whom Renoir had always admired, even though their styles seem diametrically opposed.

Returning to France by way of Marseille, he was immobilized by an attack of pneumonia at L'Estaque, where he had gone to meet Cézanne. His friend took care of him with incredible devotion. Renoir then returned to Algeria for his convalescence. During his absence the seventh Impressionist exhibition was held. He did not want to take part: "To exhibit with Pissarro, Gauguin, and Guillaumin is like exhibiting with a clique, the public does not like anything that smells of politics and I do not want to be a revolutionary at my age." But Durand-Ruel, who was organizing it, showed twenty-five paintings by Renoir which belonged to his gallery. The next year, he presented a retrospective and showed the artist's canvases abroad, in London, Boston, and Berlin.

During those tormented times, the unity of the Impressionist group was no longer what it had been. Renoir was reproached for showing at the Salon, for adapting to the taste of his middle-class customers. Degas rebuked him: "So you are working for high finance now? You will be making a tour of the country houses with Monsieur Charles Ephrussi. You will soon be exhibiting at the Mirlitons like Monsieur Bouguereau." In short, the brotherly atmosphere of the heroic days had disappeared, even if some true friendships – with Monet, Cézanne, and Caille-botte – had survived.

Piled on top of those tensions were several losses: 1883 was the year of the death of Cabaner, his gay, whimsical friend, and of Manet. His friendship for Renoir and Mallarmé was car-ried on by his brother Eugène Manet and his wife Berthe Morisot, but his col-leagues would miss the intellectual fer-ment which he had brought to their dis-cussions. Renoir's work of the time is marked by a kind of lack of continuity. The canvases he painted in Jersey and Guernsey in 1883 which, he finds: "look more like a landscape by Watteau than reality," still have their roots in Impressionism, but they also have an evanescence which is almost like Whistler. Moreover, his handling had become more classical, as witness some of the portraits of the Bérards. Renoir was plunged in a doubt which was not even dis-sipated in late 1883 by a trip to the French and Italian Rivieras with Monet or by a few days spent with Cézanne. A prey to attacks of depression, he destroyed his pic-tures: "Around 1883 there was a kind of break in my work; I had gone to the limits of Impressionism and I had reached the conclusion that I could neither paint nor draw. In a word, I was at a dead end," he confided later to Ambroise Vollard. Anxious, dissat-isfied, he dreamed of founding an association of irregulars. "Nature abhors regularity... and in their output the great artists have always been careful not to transgress that principle," he proclaimed. Hence his project to draft a pictorial, aesthetic, and theoretical grammar.

The idea occurred to him while he was reading *A Treatise on Painting* by Cennino Cennini. Franc-Lamy had come across this work by a

Polychrome bust of Aline Charigot (Musée d'Orsay, Paris), which shows Renoir's taste for sculpture.

contemporary of Fra Angelico at a second-hand bookseller's. Its evocation of the spiritual and technical aspects of painting had confirmed Renoir in his concern to be above all a good craftsman. He sought to create works with a more precise arrangement and in order to do so he revisited the Ingres in the Louvre, hunted for the memory of Corot at La Rochelle, allowed himself to be influenced by the mania for Japanese style which had been spread for twenty-five years by the Goncourt brothers, Burty, and the beautiful Judith Gautier, Théophile's daughter. In the style of those prints so prized by collectors, his new manner emphasizes the contors and uses slabs of color. *Dance in the City, The Umbrellas, The Children's Afternoon at Wargemont*, composed in a stricter, more classical style, herald the period which the critics have labelled the "hard" or "Ingres" period.

In the summer of 1885, the Renoirs rented a house at La Roche-Guyon, where they were joined by the Cézannes. The far more constructivist style of his colleague and friend from Aix infused Renoir's landscapes with a degree of discipline. In September came the first stay at Essoyes and the pursuit of an agonizing artistic quest. During those years of investigation and hesitation, "I had," he confided, "undertaken large pictures of girls bathing on which I floundered about for three years." Those *Bathers* from the Philadelphia Museum, inspired by a bas-relief by Girardon in Versailles, are the apotheosis of the Ingres style. They stirred up numerous controversies between partisans and detractors of the new manner. Berthe Morisot had seen the preliminary studies and had noted: "I don't think it is possible to go any further in the rendering of form in a drawing. For me, those nude women going into the sea are no less charming than Ingres'." Thanks to the tact of Madame Charpentier, the canvas was hung at the International Exhibition of 1887, where Monet and Whistler also had paintings on show; it was held in the sumptuous gallery of Georges Petit, Durand-Ruel's great rival. Durand-Ruel complained later that he could not find any buyers for Renoir's new manner and he urged him to abandon it. He was in the process of trying to take Impressionism to the United States, where his first exhibition in 1886 included thirty-eight paintings by Renoir.

In the same year the Impressionist group held its eighth and last exhibition. Seurat, Signac, and Pissarro revealed a new artistic orientation, neo-Impressionism, dominated by its key work *Sunday Afternoon at La Grande-Jatte*. Odilon Redon represented Symbolism, and Gauguin would soon be turning to new horizons. Renoir was not there, too absorbed in his research, his new loves, and the change of life that they brought in their wake.

The artist had a passion for moving house. Montmartre, Pigalle, and Les Batignolles swarmed with studios; his were in the Rue de Laval, where Degas lived, the Boulevard de Clichy, the Villa des Beaux-Arts, today the Rue Hégésippe Moreau, the Villa des Arts (Rue Hélène), and the Rue Tourlaque (in the same building as Suzanne Valadon and Zandomeneghi). One of the notes Mallarmé sent him through the post was written in these words:

"Villa des Arts, near the Avenue
De Clichy, where Monsieur Renoir,
Painting a bare shoulder,
Is not working with the blues."

Since he had been living with Aline, he had moved to Rue Houdon (1885), Boulevard Rochechouart (1886), and in 1889, Rue Girardon, high up in Montmartre with its gardens and orchards it still kept the appearance of a village. He occupied a pavilion of an 18th century folly, the Château des Brouillards. The place was inhabited by a small Bohemian world which catered to all his tastes: a flautist from the Opera, the novelist Paul Alexis, Georges Izambard (Rimbaud's former teacher), the member of parliament and poet Clovis Hugues. Their wives and daughters make frequent appearances in his canvases, as do the Vary sisters, who posed for him and Toulouse-Lautrec.

"You can paint so well at Les Batignolles," Renoir gibed to nettle Gauguin, who was leaving for Tahiti in 1891. However, he himself took great pleasure in moving. The country atmosphere of Essoyes was very much to his taste. There he "painted peasant girls to avoid the over-priced models of Paris," but the somewhat mannered grace of his grape-pickers or washerwomen was reminiscent of the women of Montmartre. It was there that he bought a house in 1897, and he also expressed a wish to be buried there.

This engraving of the couple in Dance at Bougival *(National Library, Paris) shows Renoir's mastery of drawing.*

The painter was often to be found at Louveciennes, as he helped to support his mother and elder brother Victor, or at Petit-Gennevilliers, at Caillebotte's house. His old friend Murer had just kept a *pied-à-terre* in Paris so as to be able to buy a mansion in Rouen and build a house in Auvers-sur-Oise. Renoir stopped by from time to time. In 1888, Cézanne invited him to Jas de Bouffan, but his stay there was short; exasperated by the miserliness of his hosts, he moved to Martigues, on the shores of Lake Berre. Once a month the dinners at the Café Riche were gatherings of the Impressionists and their friends. The Eugène Manets also received some of them – Mallarmé, Degas, Renoir, Monet from time to time – at their house in Paris, or at their country home at Mézy in 1890, then at Le Mesnil. Renoir and Manet's sister-in-law were linked by long years of mutual regard; he often went to work outdoors by her house, bringing along his models, who posed for him the different versions of *Girls in the Meadow,* which are so deliciously Proustian.

A certain stability and a return to a less dry manner followed the years of uncertainty and experiment which had led him to refuse to take part in the Universal Exhibition of 1889, when he declared: "I find everything I do bad and it would be even more distressing for me to see it on show." *Catulle Mendès' Daughters at Their Piano* was the sign both of his return to the Salon (1890) and, owing to the lack of success of the painting, of his farewell to the hard style. In January he accepted the invitation from the Cercle des XX, a great European avant-garde movement, putting up with the fact that the exhibition in Brussels was more in harmony with the Divisionism of Seurat and Signac than with his own research.

THE MOTHER-OF-PEARL PERIOD OR THE RETURN TO CHARM

The 1890s saw him return to an interpretation which was more in tune with his temperament. His brush caresses the sweetest light, the softest colors. Maurice Denis speaks of his "bouquets of women and flowers." Whether in the fields or at the piano, his girls are immersed in an idyllic setting, somewhat in the spirit of the 18th century which he venerated. It is the "mother-of-pearl" period, illustrated by a series of bathers, drowned in long hair, languid and voluptuous: *In the Meadow*, *Bathers with Long Hair*, *Girls beside the Sea*.

What a contrast with the physical and moral state of the painter, which the critic André Mellerio described in these words in 1889: "An emaciated, restless, original face to tempt the engraver, hollow cheeks and a bare forehead with bulging veins... a thin body, long fingers, Renoir is essentially nervous."

Lestringuez, Lhote, Franc-Lamy, and Zandomeneghi were witnesses at his marriage to Aline in April 1890. Always ready to receive her husband's friends, Aline also adored going away on journeys and accompanied him on his trips to the South, where he hoped to find relief for his multiple arthritis which, foreshadowed in 1888 by a facial neuralgia, was becoming increasingly painful.

During the summer of 1889, the painter rented the Montbriant property from Cézanne's brother-in-law. As at La Roche-Guyon, the rigor of the master from Aix was not without its influence. Cézanne, more spiritual, constructs, cuts up; Renoir, more sensitive, fuses, softens, shades. In 1891, the symbolist writer Teodor de Wyzeva, one of the most cultured spirits of his day, accompanied him to Tamaris-sur-Mer. Brittany, where the art world flocked, lured him back again and he stayed at Pornic and Pont-Aven in 1892 and 1893.

The rude primitivism whose echo Gauguin had found on those shores did not touch him. As always he brought along his own artistic universe, all serenity, so different from his anxious character of which Edmond Maître remarked: "When Renoir is gay, which is unusual..."

The major retrospective (110 works) held in 1892 at Durand-Ruel's brought him a host of new admirers. The most important one was Paul Gallimard, the owner of the Théâtre des Variétés, who asked him to do several portraits of his friend, the actress Jeanne Dieterle.

The stays in the French countryside were complemented by journeys abroad. Spain in 1892, where he was taken by Paul

In June 1885, while Renoir and Aline were staying at Essoyes with their son Pierre, who had been born in March, the painter did various sketches of mother and child in the garden. A page from the sketchbook has been conserved at the National Library in Paris.

The head of Claude Renoir, nicknamed Coco (Musée Renoir, Cagnes-sur-Mer). At that time, Renoir did a number of pictures expressing the affectionate, and often conspiratorial, relationships between his son and the young woman who looked after him.

Gallimard, who often invited him to Normandy; Germany in 1896, to attend Wagner's *Ring* in Bayreuth and visit the museum in Dresden; Belgium and Holland in 1896, to see Rembrandt.

Two exhibitions in 1895 showed the paths to be taken by young artists: Monet's cathedrals series at Durand-Ruel's gallery and the first exhibition devoted to Cézanne, organized by a new art-dealer, Vollard, whom Renoir had just met. Renoir, who had always believed in his old friend's talent, was full of enthusiasm. At the beginning of the year Berthe Morisot had died of influenza, barely two years after her husband. Renoir took care of the retrospective with Degas and Monet and with Mallarmé tried to amuse her daughter and her Gobillard nieces, Paule and Jeannie, who was later to marry Paul Valéry.

An addition to his family came in 1894, another boy, Jean. His godfather was a son of Durand-Ruel and his godmother was Jeanne Baudot, a student of Renoir's, the favorite companion of his painting campaigns, both in Louveciennes and in the South. He took the girls he referred to as "the little Manets" to Brittany: Bénodet, Tréboul, Pont-Aven in 1895, and to Berneval in 1898 to a chalet which had previously been occupied by Oscar Wilde. They also came to visit him at Essoyes, where he bought a house in 1895. It was there that he broke an arm in 1897 when he fell off his bicycle. He had already had a similar accident in 1880; it was the cause of a good deal of future suffering.

Other good friends died at that time, among them Norbert Goeneutte and Gustave Caillebotte. In 1894 Renoir, who had been appointed executor of Caillebotte's will, had to spend years fighting, with the aid of Martial Caillebotte, his friend's brother, to have his legacy of Impressionist paintings accepted by the nation.

Renoir had lost his mother in 1896. The death of Mallarmé in 1898 broke another link with the past. The South seemed to suit his health much better. He had adored Saint-Chamas. "If you would like to see the most beautiful country in the world," he had written to Berthe Morisot, "here it is. You have Italy, Greece, and Les Batignolles all together by the sea." But the discovery of Cagnes in 1898, thanks to a colleague from the Impressionist exhibitions, fired him with enthusiasm. He returned there from 1899 on with Jeanne Baudot.

Nonetheless, in 1900, 1901, and 1902 he tried other spots: Magagnosc, near Grasse, Le Trayas, Le Cannet. But he finally returned in 1903 and rented the "Maison de la Poste" before building the dwelling of his dreams in 1907 amidst the fine landscape of Les Collettes.

PAINTING IN THE FACE OF SUFFERING

At the turn of the century his price tag, like Monet's, was rising steadily. Sisley, who was a little jealous, had distanced himself from them ten years or so before his death (1899). Renoir's success spilled over the borders. He exhibited in the United States, in Germany, and in Russia. In 1900, for the second time, the Universal Exhibition recognized Impressionism: eleven paintings represented Renoir at the Centennial. At the age of fifty-nine the painter accepted the Légion d'Honneur, which he had refused in 1890, and justified himself in a letter to Monet, who had always had an aversion to official rewards.

In 1904, the Salon d'Automne, of which he became honorary president in 1907, devoted a room with thirty-five paintings to him. The following year, the great Impressionist exhibition in London included fifty-nine of his works. Between 1903 and 1907, a series of nudes on cushions evoked the acuteness with which he had gazed in Madrid at Titian's *Venus and Cupid with an Organist* and in London at the *The Toilet of Venus* (the Rokeby Venus) by Velázquez. Those limpid nudes came at a time when the Fauves were beginning to make themselves talked about and Cubism was taking shape. But his own enthusiasts demanded only "bathers." They also bought his small still lifes of fruit and flowers, sketches done when a more serious work became too painful for the painter.

At the beginning of the new century, his taste for youth and the warm atmosphere created by his wife Aline filled his succession of houses with life. He was as happy at Essoyes, where he was joined by the caricaturist Faivre and the sculptor Maillol, as in the South, where he found the petulant Gabrielle, who had come in 1894 to take care of Jean and would be a model to hand at Les Collettes. A third son, Claude, born when the painter was sixty, became his favorite subject, after his other sons. Old friends, like Rivière, came to Cagnes. Monet passed through in 1908. A whole new generation too: Maurice Denis, Louis Valtat, Georges d'Espagnat, and Albert André, who invited him to Laudun. His dealers, old and new, also took the road to Provence;

Renoir in 1915. Monet wrote to Georges Durand-Ruel: "I must say that Renoir is amazing. He is supposed to be seriously ill and suddenly we find out that in spite of that he is working valiantly. He is simply admirable."

Renoir painting in the garden at the Maison de la Poste in Cagnes-sur-Mer, around 1905. His son Jean explained that his father said that when he saw the state his hands were in, he used to make juggling motions to keep them agile enough to paint.

Durand-Ruel, Vollard, and Bernheim. He painted portraits of their beautiful fiancées in 1901.

Glory, but suffering too. After the first cures in 1899 at Aix-les-Bains, the illness worsened, from recurrences to terrible relapses. From 1910, Renoir was confined to an armchair, his fingers twisted by rheumatism. The man fought and painted. "Renoir is in the same sad state, but his character is always amazing. He has to be carried everywhere by two people. What torture. And even so, the same happiness when he can paint," wrote an astonished Durand-Ruel.

People begged him to paint portraits. For him it was a torment, even when he admired his model, like the exquisite Misha Godebska. He had known her since the time when she was married to Thadée Natanson and was the dream of the painters of the *Revue Blanche*, of which her husband was the director. Renoir owed Misha one of his last artistic emotions. She was then the wife of the wealthy Edwards and patroness of the Ballets Russes. In 1911, the old painter, half paralyzed, watched one of their spectacular performances from her box, which fully gratified his taste for color.

He had become completely helpless and had to rent an apartment in Nice to have a studio accessible. His success was international by then: "I could do anything, I just have to sign," he grumbled. To please Vollard, the painter embarked on sculpture in 1913 at Essoyes; he had some works made by Richard Guino, a pupil of Maillol.

The end of his life was darkened by the First World War. Shortly before, Gabrielle had left to marry the American painter Conrad Slade. His eldest sons were called up and wounded. His wife died in 1915, after she had been to see Jean at the front. Nevertheless, Renoir continued to travel between Paris, Essoyes, Louveciennes, and Les Collettes, where Matisse came to visit him in 1917. His last big outing was in 1919, a visit to the Louvre, which the director opened specially for him. By then, Renoir was a national treasure.

Crippled with pain, the artist only thought of depicting the freshness of youth. The more his body twisted up, the more his brush expressed the freedom of female forms. "His women are enchantresses. If you brought one home, she would be the person you would look at last before leaving and first on returning, she would fill a place in your life," said Duret. Nudes, landscapes, mythological evocations, there is a kind of jubilation on his palette. His canvases flame with saffrons, blues, reds, like the *Bathers* donated by his sons to the Louvre. The model for the last ones was Andrée, who was to marry Jean Renoir and act under the name of Catherine Hessling. The man who had so loved the theatre had an actor son, Pierre Renoir, and an actress daughter-in-law, Colonna Romano. Jean was to become a film director. Claude, whom he had taught his first occupation, ceramics, would himself have a son who was a film technician. To all of them he has passed on his passion for the image.

"I don't think I have ever spent a day without painting," Renoir said on the eve of his death. On 2 December 1919 he called for his brushes to paint a bouquet of flowers. Once the work was finished, he murmured: "I think I'm beginning to see something in it." A few hours later, Pierre-Auguste Renoir died at Les Collettes at the age of seventy-eight. At the end of fifty years' work the artist for whom happiness and painting were one and the same thing left behind him about a thousand works.

In the book dedicated to his father in 1962, Jean Renoir describes how he recalls him at the turn of the century: "What surprised people who did not know him and were seeing him for the first time were his eyes and his hands... For his expression, imagine a mixture of irony and tenderness, of humour and voluptuousness... Perhaps it was all a mask. For Renoir was very prudish and did not like to show the emotions that seized him when he was looking at flowers, women, the clouds in the sky... He did not look a man of our time; he reminded us of a monk from the Italian Renaissance."

LE CABARET DE LA MÈRE
ANTONY, 1866
Oil on canvas, 195 x 130 cm
Nationalmuseum, Stockholm

LE CABARET DE LA MÈRE ANTONY

In this work of Renoir's youth, the people are treated, not without a certain naivety, in the manner of the Dutch group portraits of the 17th century, from which he takes the dark range – black, brown, dark blue – which makes the faces stand out and gives precision to their expressions. This is no middle-class dining-room with starchy guests and sumptuous tableware; we are at a country inn, the inn of Mère Antony, at Marlotte, the meeting place where the landscape painters who have come to work in the Forest of Fontainebleau gather in the evening. The clothes of the actors in this scene are just like the ones the artists wore when working outdoors: velvet suit or thick linen smock. Renoir's painting breathes comradeship and serenity. Nevertheless, on the wall in the background the caricatures and notes of

music drawn by the passing art students identify this peaceful spot, in case anyone is unaware of it, as the gayest of Bohemian rendezvous. Renoir himself had sketched the silhouette of Murger high up on the wall. The author of *Scènes de la vie de Bohème*, the bible of all young artists, seems to be following the conversation around the table with interest. This slightly off-centre pyramidal composition is structured by the direction of the glances, which draw a diagonal from the ghostly Murger to the very real man in the white panama hat whose companions seem to be drinking in his words. The lack of direct information makes it impossible to identify these three characters with certainty. The one standing is probably Jules Le Cœur; seated facing us, most likely a man called Bosc (or Bos); and, with his back turned, probably Sisley. Their discussion is of no interest to either the innkeeper, wearing the knotted neckerchief so typical of French peasant women on her head, or the waitress, Nana, a name that was to be made famous by Zola.

The poodle lying the foreground seems to be looking at the painter working on the scene outside the field of the picture.

A remarkable interaction of different shades of white – the tablecloth, the apron, the crockery – focuses attention on the centre of the canvas. We could also isolate, like the elements of a still life, the cups, the plates, the fruit, painted with a

committed realism expressed by the dirty napkins and the apple with a bite taken out of it. The essential element, however, is the newspaper with the title carefully placed to be read: *L'Événement*. That daily was indeed at the core of all the conversations of Renoir and his friends, since Zola, who had been commissioned to write about the Salon, had lambasted official painting and penned a plea in favor of Manet and their group. With its slightly rustic naturalism and its host of implications, this picture, which Renoir was to recall with pleasure years later, looks today like a large souvenir photograph.

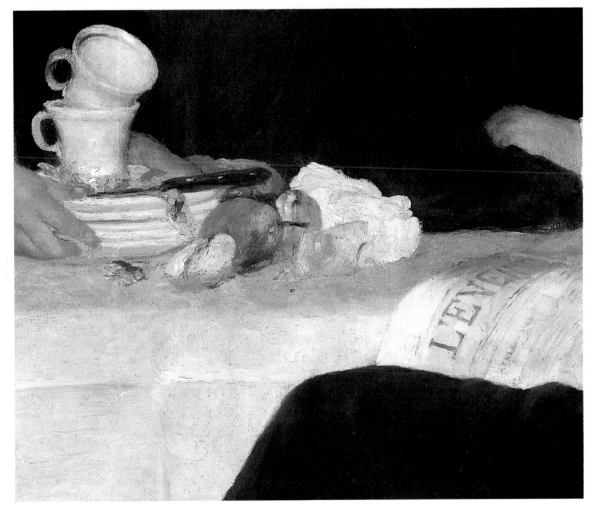

BAZILLE PAINTING AT HIS EASEL, 1867
Oil on canvas, 105 x 73 cm
Musée d'Orsay (Marc Bazille Bequest), Paris

BAZILLE PAINTING AT HIS EASEL

Painted in the cold, even light of the studio, this picture – still realistic in style – is treated in extremely subtle harmonies of gray. They are picked out with ochre, which endows the whole painting with that fair tonality recommended to his pupils by Corot, whom Bazille had met at Chailly. Frédéric Bazille, one of Renoir's closest friends, was one of the pivots of the emerging Impressionist group. Generous, warm-hearted and talented, he died at the age of 29 in the Franco-Prussian War of 1870, leaving sixty or so works behind him.

Most portraits show the model face on. Here we see Bazille in profile: an original attitude designed to display the artist's concentration on his work. The fineness of the brush shows that he is putting the finishing touches to a work which is practically complete.

The intelligent composition is based on horizontal or vertical rectangles: the canvases hung on the wall, the palette and the picture resting on the easel. Their

straight lines contrast with the broken ones of the drawing of Bazille's body. As we admire this discreet science of layout, we may recall that Renoir had competed successfully at the Beaux-Arts on the subject of putting different objects in perspective. This work, a standard example of the picture within a picture, is also a microcosm of the relations between the painters. When he painted it, in 1867, Renoir was sharing Bazille's studio (in the Rue Visconti). Monet joined them in March, bringing his first snowy landscapes from Honfleur.

We can recognize one of them, *The Road to Saint-Siméon*, hanging on the wall. Initiates know that another painter, Sisley, who does not appear in this painting, was nevertheless working in the studio at the same time. The still life that Bazille, in his slippers, is finishing off, depicts a heron and jays. Sisley is working at his side on the same subject, which he entitled *Heron with Outspread Wings*. The museum in Montpellier, the town of Bazille's birth, has the two canvases. It seems that

the likeness of this portrait was striking. Bazille's father would be happy to exchange it for *Women in the Garden* which his son had bought from Monet three years before his death.

SUMMER, ALSO CALLED LISE OR LA BOHÉMIENNE, 1868
Oil on canvas, 85 x 59 cm
Nationalgalerie, Staatliche Museen, Berlin

SUMMER, ALSO CALLED LISE OR LA BOHÉMIENNE

Summer, the true title which Renoir gave this canvas, is particularly revealing. Through this portrait one of the essential concerns of Impressionism begins to emerge: the transcription of notations of atmosphere. The question for the painter here is to render the feeling of the dampness of summer. He succeeds completely. The girl in the picture, Lise Tréhot, was the daughter of a postmaster whom Renoir met at the house of his painter friend Jules Le Cœur. She would be his model and mistress, posing for most of his paintings until 1872. A perfect example of a naturalism which shuns excess, the work is constructed on a very simple pattern: a young girl sitting, facing us, her hands demurely clasped, stands out from a background of greenery. The novel element is the background, a dense foliage hastily sketched with disordered brush strokes and dotted with holes of dazzling light. However, the brush is wielded with care for the face and the bust, which the painter has given an almost photographic appearance.

This young woman is scantily dressed; only a light bodice and a striped skirt. There is no erotic undertone, though, unlike the *Young Women on the Banks of the Seine*, the work with which Courbet had created a scandal at the Salon in 1857.

Her hair in disorder, a ring in her ear, this so-called Bohemian, who seems to be striking something of a studio pose, could be a cousin of Victor Hugo's Esmeralda. Renoir had exhibited a painting illustrating *Notre-Dame de Paris* in 1864, but it bears no resemblance to *La Petite Bohémienne*, that wild creature, so refined and bold, that Renoir would paint ten years later near Dieppe. The green of the leaves acts as a complement to the dominance of the reds, making them even more striking. Reds which are echoed from the ribbon to

the lips and taken up again in the stripes of the skirt. The absent gaze, the bowed shoulders and the feverish cheeks speak of the exhaustion of a day of heat and a long drawn-out posing session.

Though the picture was accepted by the Salon in 1869, the hanging committee did not consider the subject elevated enough for it to be hung in a place of honor. But some years later Edgar Degas praised it so highly to Théodore Duret that he bought it on the spot. In his *Histoire des Peintres Impressionnistes*, the first of the countless works devoted to the movement, Duret considered this *Bohémienne* as Renoir's debut "in the field of open-air painting."

BOY WITH CAT, 1868
Oil on canvas, 124 x 67 cm
Musée d'Orsay, Paris

BOY WITH CAT

Renoir tackles this
classical subject (the male
nude) from a modern point
of view. Instead of
representing the model in a
heroic pose, like David's
Romans in *The
Intervention of the Sabine
Women* or Ingres' Greeks
in *The Envoys from
Agamemnon*, Renoir
depicts him in a posture
which is more homely than
glorious. He chooses a
moment when the model is
relaxing. The slightly loose
stance, the gentle
movement formed by the
circle of the arms and
the ecstatic expression
of the cat which we can
almost hear purring
underline the impression
of abandon. But if the
upper part of the body
leaning on the table
speaks of repose, the left
foot resting on the toes
imbues the scene with the
instantaneous character
which the Impressionists
always seek to convey.
In spite of the penumbra,
the face is drawn with
particular care: the marked
eyebrow, the strong nose,
the voluptuous mouth
and the black hair which
accentuates the pallor of
the body. The features
of this young boy whose
name we do not know
incline us to think that he
is one of the Italian models
paid four francs an hour to

pose for the studios and academies of Montmartre or the Latin Quarter. But most of all it is the dazzling nakedness of this ephebe that Renoir, always anxious to render the glow of skin, whether of a man or a woman, brings to the fore. The body poised between childhood and manhood stands out against a dark background. The vertical line and the austere nakedness are in contrast to the shimmering richness of the fabric. A diffuse sensuality, stripped of all ambiguity, radiates from that cloth where tactile sensations are subtly conveyed. Renoir's brush caresses to render the cat's silky fur,

the velvet of an adolescent skin, the softness of the green cushion, the satin of the material.
Another element which heralds the Renoir of the future is the treatment of the sumptuous tablecloth. Touches of blue and white endow this satin damask with a life of its own, a shimmer which we find years later in the women's clothes reproduced with such virtuosity by the painter.

SKATERS IN THE BOIS DE BOULOGNE, 1868
Oil on canvas, 72 x 92 cm
Private Collection

SKATERS IN THE BOIS DE BOULOGNE

With this painting, Renoir is tipping over into a different conception of reality: the fleeting impression seized for the first time with all its instantaneous quality. The painter is installed in a restaurant in the Bois de Boulogne. Transformed into an English style garden by Haussmann and Davioud, it had become one of the favourite haunts of fashionable Paris.

Unlike Monet or Berthe Morisot, Renoir painted few winter landscapes, explaining towards the end of his life to his dealer Ambroise Vollard: "I could never stand the cold and, besides, why paint snow, that sickness of nature?" The success of the Dutch painter Jongkind with scenes of this kind, so typical of his country, may well have something to do with this sudden interest in skating. The movement of

the scene springs from the freedom of the drawing. In this crowd, each character is captured in a completely real and gently ironic attitude. Three brush strokes are enough to portray the waiter, the sweeper, the skaters, skillful or clumsy, shivering with cold or bursting with confidence. Illustrated magazines show identical scenes, but here there is a lack of artistic constraint which is a step towards a total transformation of painting.

The novelty lies in the feeling of animation. There is nothing static about the picture; on the contrary, silhouettes seem to be dancing against a leaden sky in a diffuse light which rises up from the ice. On the left-hand side, the foliage of the black pine is treated with those rounded velvety brush strokes that Renoir would use forty years later in his views of Cagnes. The range of colors, still sober, is very refined. The snow is tinged with ochre in the foreground, shows hints of blue in the shadow and is a dazzling white in the full light. This effect involves a clever spacing of elements between the empty chair (at the front of the scene) and the downy line of trees streaking the horizon.

The arrangement of the people in the landscape and the vibrations of light, so typical of Impressionism, are already present in this picture. One of the first "great" Renoirs.

FLOWERS IN A VASE, c. 1869
Oil on canvas, 65 x 54 cm
Museum of Fine Arts, Boston

FLOWERS IN A VASE

Flowers everywhere: in a vase, in the classical manner, growing wild in gardens, fields and orchards, Impressionist style, embroidered on a piece of material, or caressing a face, enhancing hair, overflowing on a hat. From his beginnings as a young apprentice when he painted flowers on plates to the day he died, Renoir scattered his work with roses and poppies. At this time the surge of interest in 17th century Dutch art which accompanied the spread of Realism gave a fresh impetus to still lifes and paintings of flowers in particular. But the dragonflies, butterflies and snails which, in the paintings of Van Huysum or Roelant Savery, alluded to the shortness of life, have disappeared in the work of Courbet, Manet and, most of all, Fantin-Latour. Through him Renoir found out about the commercial success of subjects of that kind in Britain. He treated them neither with the grand style of the French 17th century, as many of his contemporaries did, nor with the intellectual connotations which the Symbolists gave them, but

in the purest spirit of Naturalism.
A dark background highlights the explosion of this bouquet whose colors are vaguely echoed in a blurred tablecloth. The slightly pasty touch looks closer to Courbet than to Fantin. Those carelessly arranged flowers (dahlias, phlox, daisies, sunflowers) bloom in late summer. The picture must have been painted in September 1869 at Saint-Michel-de-Bougival, at Monet's house. Indeed, Monet himself, in a slightly different composition with more fruit, depicted the same bouquet in the same stoneware vase decorated (by Renoir?) with crescent moons. The simple layout is essentially a play on the opposition between the burst of color of the flowers at the bottom of the vase and the golden glow of the sunflowers. "Painting flowers rests my brain," Renoir said. "I do not bring the same tension of spirit as when I am working with a model."

LA GRENOUILLÈRE, 1869
Oil on canvas, 66 x 86 cm
Nationalmuseum, Stockholm

LA GRENOUILLÈRE

Here is "La Grenouillère", the most famous pleasure garden on the banks of the Seine, on the Île de Croissy. It was in this enchanting setting that Impressionism was born under the brush strokes of Renoir and Monet.
The spot was the rendezvous of the beautiful people; Renoir was taken there by Prince Bibesco. But what could have been just a scene from modern life and the world of fashion becomes, through an unprecedented process of artistic destructuring, the brilliant emergence of a new style.
The work gives the same impression of speed as a sketch, but it rests on a complex architecture, forged less by the opposition than by the fusion of the solid elements: the floating bathhouse, the natural features (tree, water) and the live actors of that sunny afternoon.
The firmness of the brush confers a certain stability on the circular contours of the islet, known as "the flowerpot" or "the camembert", joined to the bank and the floating café by gangways. A certain static quality still marks the boats moored in the foreground, but the glimmers of mahogany of the boat which the child is holding on to and its oblique position help to create the impression of motion which brings the

whole composition to life. The sky appears only through the gaps in the foliage, but its azure color is fully reflected in the river with all the variations introduced by the ripples and shadows. The water is darkened to ultramarine in the foreground of the painting and tinged, in the distance, with emerald green. The differences are created by the way the colors are applied: broad horizontal lines for the shimmer of the water or small strokes flecked with white, on the left, for the swimmers with just their heads emerging from the river. On the islet, the round stains of the leaves of the poplar seem to be rustling in the breeze. The farther we go from the shore, the more the hustle and bustle seems to fade. The downy line of trees on the far bank closes the composition, but the light touch of the sun creates a discreet effect of atmospheric perspective. Renoir did three more views of "La Grenouillère". In this version, even more than in the others, the human element is united to nature by a simple interplay of

reflections. The light-colored dresses of the "grenouilles" (frogs), those somewhat frivolous Parisian women who came to spend their Sundays by the river, contrast with the dark jackets of their companions. All the characters are suggested; no face appears distinctly. Nevertheless, they all have an intense life. Those almost sketchy figures in motion, which prompted detractors to say that the painting was not finished, that evocation of the lapping of the water, the shouts of the bathers, the breath of the breeze... Was Renoir aware that he was taking a revolutionary step? When Maupassant described "La Grenouillère" ten years later, it had gone out of fashion and he saw nothing more than "the gaiety of a bazaar." Thirty years more and it was a deserted pleasure garden that drew Apollinaire's nostalgic eye: "Neither the painters nor Maupassant stroll there... ... Little boats on the shores of the island You make me feel sorry for you."

MADAME MONET LYING ON A SOFA, 1872
Oil on canvas, 54 x 73 cm
Calouste Gulbenkian Foundation, Lisbon

MADAME MONET LYING ON A SOFA

Quiet days at Argenteuil, where the Monets often entertained Renoir in the house they had rented after the war. Camille was a ready-made model. A ravishing but ephemeral figure of an avant-garde which had yet to be given the name Impressionism, Camille was never to know the glory destined for her friends; she died in 1879 at Vétheuil. In the happy Argenteuil years, Renoir often painted her among the blooming shrubbery of the garden or in the nearby meadows.
In this picture, Madame Monet is first of all a dress in a shimmer of blue and white. But it is not a matter of showing a dress intended to highlight the silhouette of the model, but of juxtaposing colored planes to delight the eye.
This is one of the rare works where the influence of the Orient can be discerned. Renoir was less responsive than his friends to the novelty of Japanese prints which, he once gibed, are "extremely interesting provided they remain in Japan."
Edmond de Goncourt, one of the pioneers of Japanese style and fairly indifferent to the aesthetics of the Impressionists, referred to them as "sketchers, who turn out spots of color that they haven't invented. Spots stolen from Goya, spots stolen from the Japanese."
Renoir is clearly transposing those two influences here. Like Goya's *Maja vestida*, Camille, reclining on her divan, looks the spectator

in the eye. Moreover, her discreetly sinuous line and heavy black hair, the only break in the light tonality of the whole, transform the young woman into a Parisian geisha, an allusion stressed by the Japanese bowl near her hand. She is holding a newspaper (*Le Figaro*) but she is not reading it, although the canvas seizes the exact moment at which the reading is interrupted by the arrival of a visitor at whom she directs a languid gaze. The diagonal layout allows the folds of the material to undulate gently, the only hint of motion in this static composition which is so different from the artist's habitual style. It breaks as much with the naturalism of the portrait of Bazille or *La Bohémienne* as it does with the vibrations of Impressionist technique. The whites, blues and grays which shade into each other stack the embroidered ovals in a manner which is almost abstract. A single wavy line passes from the braid of the dress to the border of the sofa for a closer blending of the elements of this minimalist decor. The bulge of the cushions heightens the impression of nonchalance and intimacy. This closed universe is stamped with a lack of realism which is exceptional in Renoir's work.

**THE PARISIENNE OR LADY
IN BLUE,** 1874
Oil on canvas, 160 x 106 cm
*National Museum of Wales,
Cardiff*

THE PARISIENNE OR LADY
IN BLUE

Renoir conceived this
large, standing portrait of a
charming actress, Madame
Henriot, as the apotheosis
of blue. He was answering
the rejection the year
before by the Salon of
*Bridle Path in the Bois de
Boulogne* because of the
amount of blue it
contained.
Paris is the unchallenged
capital of fashion and this
Parisienne looks today like
an exquisite creation by
Worth or Madame La
Ferrière. It is a costume of
the kind worn by elegant
ladies on their daily stroll
in the Bois de Boulogne.
Apart from the face, not an
inch of skin is visible.
Even the neck is enclosed
in a delicate collar. The
white muslin prevents
the tone of the dress from
contaminating the face.
Renoir weaves in every
shade of blue with his
brush: lighter for the
buttons which bring out
the slenderness of the bust;
darker for a lace inset, a
flounce, a fold; bordering
on mauve for the gloves
and the hat; almost black in
the hollows of the
shadows. This range allows
him to play with the
volumes which give the
fabric its lightness and
style: he gathers in here,
there he brings out the
bustle with a clever fold.
He plays with the ribbons

which he ties around the neck and carelessly unties on the wrist. The white flash of the sleeve, with a muffled echo around the neck and in the hair, lights up the shades of blue. His father the tailor, his mother the dressmaker and his friend Sisley the son of a silk and artificial flower merchant had much to do with his knowledge of fabrics and the elegance of a garment. Renoir knows a dress which falls well. In his paintings, silks and satins have their own rhythm and are more a living element than a backdrop. The artist does not aim for the minute detail that brought Winterhalter or Stevens their success. His brush strokes remain deliberately visible. The young woman appears against one of those "nowhere backgrounds" that Renoir loved in Velazquez. He treats it with a remarkable virtuosity. Indistinct at first glance, for the attentive observer the floor, the wall and the curtain take on the almost abstract, but necessary, value of decorative elements around the central figure.

This *Parisienne* is not just a costume, however ravishing; she is also a state of mind which Renoir is determined to convey. Her ingenuous air, those curls spilling out from under her bonnet, her three-quarters pose which shows the curve of her body: everything is done to give that piquante, frivolous air which is attributed to Parisian women. When it was shown at the first Impressionist exhibition, it received some positive reviews.

An extraordinary presence emanates from this life-size portrait which was hung in London in 1979 and in Paris in 1985. Each time it fascinates the public, as if the reincarnation of an unknown young woman suddenly emerged from the blue mists.

**THE PATH THROUGH THE
LONG GRASS,** 1874
Oil on canvas, 60 x 74 cm
Musée d'Orsay, Paris

THE PATH THROUGH THE LONG GRASS

This celebration of nature, full of the freshness of springtime and joyful serenity, is fully representative of the Argenteuil period. Those broken touches, those little brush strokes that make the canvas vibrate are a perfect expression of the sensations we feel on a beautiful day: the breath of the air, the rustling of nature, the simple pleasures of a stroll in the countryside. A banal tuft of grass takes on the same value as a person and a few shades of green and yellow, punctuated with red and blue, are enough for Renoir to invent a universe.

The space, given rhythm by the waving grass in the meadow and the trembling shadows of the trees, is divided by the bright path which runs through the middle of the picture. At the top it cuts diagonally into the horizon, where the spiral of a poplar and the vibrant blotch of a lower tree stand out. The

by the slope and the proximity of the fence, while the others prefer to prolong the pleasure of the stroll.

This sloping path leads to the mill at the village of Orgemont, from where there is one of the finest views of the city of Paris. Auguste Renoir often went to meet Claude Monet there and they both worked on the same subject. Happy moments, when everyone had the feeling that he was giving the best of himself, when Impressionism was at its height.

foreground is bursting with bushes and flowers. The red poppies and the white chickweed rise at the approach of the walkers, whose sunshades and hats bring their own touches of color. On the left a series of trees, leafier but still rustling, bring shade and cool to the dazzling sunlight of that beautiful day.

On the right of *The Path through the Long Grass* a touch of blue opens up the distant landscape towards the outskirts of the capital, while the fence in the foreground – the only static element – closes off the walk.

The walkers are coming down the sloping path, which accentuates the movement, and their division into two different groups confers a sense of intimacy and an instantaneous quality on the scene. The ones at the front seem to be drawn on

TORSO IN THE SUN, 1875
Oil on canvas, 81 x 65 cm
Musée d'Orsay, Paris

TORSO IN THE SUN

Shown for the first time at the second Impressionist exhibition in 1876, this work is the quintessence of the aims that the group was pursuing. Light and reflections, the two components of the new painting, are carried to extremes. Nothing could be farther from the academic nude: the study of the torso, that subject the students at the Beaux-Arts were always being urged to paint in the unchanging light of the studios, is metamorphosed by its transfer to the open air.

The idea seems to be the same as for *La Bohémienne*: to express the sensation of summer through a female body. The pose and the setting are almost identical: a young girl, facing the spectator, her hair in disarray, against a background of vegetation. But it is not so much the nudity that makes these works so different. Instead of standing out against a symbolic background, the model in the *Torso in the Sun* blends into it in a most intimate way.

The foliage is not treated with a uniform tonality; it explodes in a burst of colors and shapes rendered by disordered brush strokes which spring out and whirl around. On the right, sheaves of gold, greens, blues and whites assault the body. On the left, shadowy ultramarines

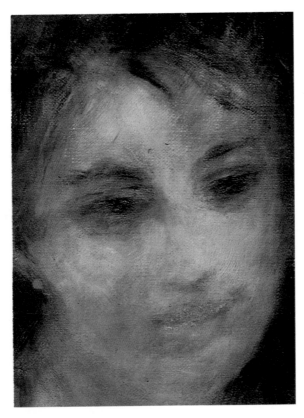

accentuate the depth of the foliage. Here and there a stroke of red lashes the greenery. In the center, enfolding the roundness of the body with a gently circular movement, a drape merges with the palpitation of the plants. The whole torso – shoulders, breasts, belly and arms – is part of the explosion of light whose subdued reflections are inscribed in stains of violet, blue or green on the watered skin.

The face also shines out from the life vibrating around it. The pinkish complexion is further underlined by the mouth and the one earring which we can see. The gaze seems absent, as if absorbed in that invasive nature. A ring and a bracelet, the only realistic elements, seem to be escaping from the profusion of vegetation.

A total incomprehension

which soon gave way to fury greeted this nude with its halo of light. "Try to explain to Monsieur Renoir that a woman's torso is not a mass of decomposing flesh with green, purplish stains that denote the state of total putrefaction of a corpse." A barb that cut to the quick: the author of the lines was Albert Wolff, the all-powerful critic of *Le Figaro*. "Your model has had smallpox," commented another journalist.

The model who was the subject of these virulent attacks was Anna, one of the girls of the Butte Montmartre whose freshness and spontaneity Renoir appreciated so much. Here, however, the miracle of Impressionist vibrations transforms her into a goddess of nature, who has emerged from the woods at the edge of a cornfield.

**FIRST EVENING OUT,
ALSO CALLED LE CAFÉ-
CONCERT,** 1876
Oil on canvas, 65 x 50 cm
The National Gallery, London

**FIRST EVENING OUT, ALSO
CALLED LE CAFÉ-CONCERT**

A passion for the theatre,
the opera or the café-
concert, was as much a
feature of Renoir as of
Degas. They brought into
fashion a theme to which
the Realists, with the
exception of Daumier, paid
little attention.
Impressionist vibrations,
the source of so many
sunlit visions, are applied
just as happily to artificial
light. Renoir delights in
painting this world with
which he is so familiar
though his liaison with
Madame Henriot.
Here he stresses the feeling
of an enclosed space in
which two planes
separated by the arc of the
side of the box mark out

with precision the territory of the main character and that of the extras. The painter frames the picture like a photograph: a close-up of the young woman whose profile lights up the whole right-hand side of the canvas, gradually going out of focus as the eye moves to the background where the fleeting silhouettes jostle together.

No impression of depth in spite of the difference of scale, as the bronze and blue tones bathe the whole setting in a general tonality. Renoir's pet color runs through its whole range of variations. The ultramarine is almost black in the dress, scarcely lit by a white cuff at the edge of the pleated flounce of the sleeve. Other, more fluid, blues mix with whites or blacks in the clothes of the audience. Navy blue also for the dress of the companion, mother, sister or governess, barely glimpsed behind the radiant heroine of the painting. And the hat, which provides a festival of cobalts lightened or darkened by greens, mauves or white.

The round bouquet of violet and yellow pansies is probably a gift from an admirer. The work is otherwise organized around three faces, whose eyes describe an invisible triangle. The face of the young girl sitting upright in the box, her position and her demure, concentrated, almost grave air, betray the emotions of this first evening out and her wonder and astonishment at the show. Two other figures emerge from the sinuous contours of the crowd, in which the people are barely sketched, but enough for us to discern pleasure and excitement: an older woman darts an envious glance at this radiant apparition of youth, while in the stalls a man (Renoir?) turns round, as if conquered by the beauty of the spectator in the hat. This delicious young person is one of those young girls in flower who would come to life a few years later by the pen of that most Impressionist of writers, Marcel Proust.

THE SWING, 1876
Oil on canvas, 92 x 73 cm
Musée d'Orsay, Paris

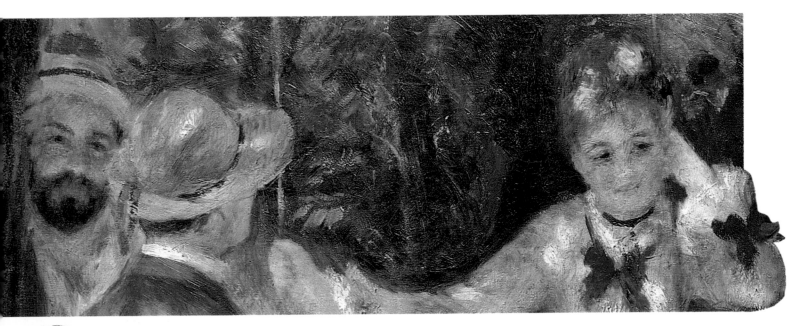

THE SWING

Painted in the marvellous garden in the Rue Cortot in Montmartre, this picture expresses the quintessence of Impressionism. First because of its subject, a scene from everyday life: three adults and a little girl grouped around a swing. Next because of its instantaneous quality: at the moment when the swing is suspended in its arc, a certain lethargy seems to have imposed itself on movement. Last, because of the extraordinary play of light and shadow: on the ground, the clothes, the hats and the hair, everywhere except for the faces, Renoir scatters stains of sunlight which produce those shadows in a violet which people at the time, who were used to black shadows, found scandalous.

The play of expressions and attitudes helps to create the slightly unreal atmosphere that emerges from the painting. No glances are exchanged: the man with his back turned and the little girl, an admiring glow in her eyes, are looking at the young woman (Jeanne, one of his Montmartre models). But she is looking away, with a dreamy expression in her eyes. The nonchalant movement of the head, resting on the rope, adds still more to the feeling of languor. The man leaning on the tree trunk (the painter Norbert Goeneutte) is also looking at something outside the scene. Each one of them seems to be immersed in a peaceful daydream.

And yet what stormy reactions this peaceful work was to unleash at the third Impressionist exhibition in 1877. The critic of *L'Événement* denounced "those effects of sunlight combined in such a bizarre fashion that they look exactly like spots of grease on people's clothes." The inspector of the Beaux-Arts, Ballu, found "the struggle with nature ridiculous." However, the partisans of the new school were enthusiastic. "We have to go back to Watteau to find charm of the kind that impregnates *The Swing*," exclaimed Georges Rivière. Another tribute, from Zola, who in his novel *A Love Affair* (1878), was inspired by the scene to describe his heroine: "Standing on the swing, her arms outstretched holding the ropes... she wore a gray dress decorated with mauve ribbons."

DANCE AT THE MOULIN DE LA GALETTE, 1876
Oil on canvas, 131 x 175 cm
Musée d'Orsay, Paris

DANCE AT THE MOULIN DE LA GALETTE

This famous painting brought glory not only to its author, but to Montmartre. With *Dance at the Moulin-Rouge* by Toulouse-Lautrec, it created the legendary image that brings tourists from all over the world flocking to this hill in Paris.
What better occasion than a dance in the open air to portray everything Renoir loved: the bright light of a sunny afternoon, the sinuous movements of a crowd swept along by the dance, the furtive or conspicuous elegance of a silhouette, the expression on a face and, most of all, the intense joy of living exuded by a popular holiday occasion.
Renoir achieves a perfect integration of an almost classical perspective with the tachiste style of blots of color which portray all the elements of the picture, whose touches of light, so typical of the period, model the forms. The all light composition retreats towards the background with the movement of the dance. Various diagonals help to create this effect. One passes through the two women dancing, dressed in pink and blue, another along the backs of the benches. Yet another links the boatmen's black ribbons with the straw hat decorated with red. In the background, the green vault of the trees closes off the scene with a horizontal line broken vertically by the white stems of the lamp-posts.
To paint this picture, the most ambitious one of the decade, Renoir rented a studio just a step away from the "Moulin de la Galette" – it took its name from the cakes that were served there – where, in a shady garden, a public composed of families rather than riff-raff came to dance polkas and quadrilles.
All the local people from the hill posed willingly for this *Dance*, which today looks like the *Embarkation for Cythera* of the Impressionist

generation. Renoir also presents all his inseparable companions. Georges Rivière, a lifelong friend, lists the heroes and heroines. In the foreground two sisters, Estelle and Jeanne, in Watteau-style dresses; then Franc-Lamy, Goeneutte, and Rivière himself "seated at a table with glasses of the traditional blackcurrant syrup." Gervex, Cordey, Lestringuez, Lhote, and others appear among the dancers. Lastly, a painter of Spanish origin who had come from Cuba, Don Pedro Vidal de Solares y Cardenas, is dancing with Margot, Renoir's favorite model since 1875. All the others are painters, with the exception of Lestringuez, a civil servant and passionate enthusiast of occultism.

Psychologically the work rests on the contrast between two distinct phases: the dance (left and centre) and repose (foreground and right). The couples whirling in a powdering of light are contrasted with the seated groups, a darker mass where the exchange of glances replaces the movement of the bodies. A whole range of emotions can be read on the faces: excitement, seduction, expectation, curiosity, fatigue. The brush is fluid, the contours scarcely marked, the stretches of sunlight alternate with blue shadows and the palette is lit up by the light dresses of the women. The touches of light play on the clothes, the faces, bounce off the hats or the back of a chair. Sometimes a couple is isolated by a shaft of light from a projector; thus Cardenas and Margot seem to be dancing on a cloud of violet shadows. The eye is drawn towards a more blurred background, where heads and silhouettes, brushed in with quick strokes, evoke the confusion of a crowd in motion. Unveiled at the third Impressionist exhibition in 1877, the painting aroused admiration and astonishment. An enthusiastic Caillebotte bought it and proclaimed that he "would not exchange it for the Venus by Bouguereau," the idol of the bourgeois public of the day.

**CHILD WITH
WATERING CAN,** 1876
Oil on canvas, 100 x 73 cm
*National Gallery of Art (Chester
Dale Collection), Washington*

CHILD WITH WATERING CAN

Famous or unknown, the children painted by Renoir all bear witness to his genius as a portraitist. Unlike a Goya, who depicts the slightly cruel ambiguity of childhood, Renoir, faithful to his temperament and his admiration for Baudelaire, prefers to evoke "the green paradise of childhood love." Before the commissions that almost engulfed him in later years, this portrait is one of those total expressions of his pleasure in painting. What is more banal than a child in a park? And yet the subtle harmony of the garden which seems to have been created specially for the little girl, her air of innocence and absolute confidence in life, endow the canvas with a sense of eternity.

Once again we admire the care taken by the painter with the clothes: the embroidery drawn in minute detail, the alignment of the buttons, the bootees. This outfit, which looks so refined to us today, was quite standard for its period. The dress plays a primary role in the composition here. With its strong geometry and the navy blue which breaks with the palette of light colors, it imposes the little girl as the central element of the picture. A corner of lawn, a path, a discreet shrubbery, the setting humbles itself before childhood.

Renoir, who allowed his little models to come and go as they pleased, excels in the art of capturing the grace of an attitude or a fleeting expression on a face: the watering can which the little girl is holding as if it were a treasure and her face which expresses a mixture of the pleasure and the seriousness of the task. An undeniable virtuosity is combined with a subtle perception of the first years of life, whether his models look like princesses, as in *Les Demoiselles Cahen d'Anvers* (1881), wild creatures, as in *La Petite Bohémienne* (1879), or well-behaved children, as in *Martial Caillebotte 's Children* (1895).

The red ribbon in the hair could be a reference to Velazquez. "The little pink ribbon of the Infanta Marguerita contains the whole art of painting," the painter avowed while looking at the masterpiece in the Louvre. As if in answer, Jules Renard expressed his admiration for Renoir: "We look and his little girls' mouths break into a gentle smile!... and those eyes that open like flowers!"

MADAME CHARPENTIER AND HER CHILDREN, 1878
Oil on canvas, 153.7 x 190.2 cm
The Metropolitan Museum of Art (Wolfe Fund-1907, C. Lorillard Wolfe Collection), New York

MADAME CHARPENTIER AND HER CHILDREN

A portrait of Madame Charpentier was not to be hung just anywhere. The juries of the Salon of 1879 were well aware of the fact. The daughter of one of Napoleon III's jewellers, the wife of the man who published the Naturalist writers, received in her drawing-room everyone who was anyone in the Paris of arts, letters, theatre and politics.

This large format painting brought Impressionism into the Salon in triumph and, thanks to the contacts he had made at the Charpentiers' house, Renoir saw the orders flowing in. "I think he is launched," wrote Pissarro,

"thank heaven! Poverty is so hard."

This time the setting is not limited to a cascade of greenery or a few hangings in an anonymous room. Madame Charpentier is depicted in her Japanese boudoir, a choice which reveals the infatuation of the mistress of the house with Japanese style. Against the wall the kakemonos bathe the room with a brick red and gold tonality. Another warm touch, provided by the combination of the cane chair and the glowing still life of flowers, fruit, a decanter and pieces of Venetian glass.

The horizontal format accentuates the intimate quality of the room. The Impressionism is restricted to the pieces of furniture; the people are treated with an almost classical virtuosity. No inopportune brush stroke troubles the porcelain faces, the velvet, the turquoise taffetas. The central element of the painting, Madame Charpentier embodies the classical figure of the Mother, protective and severe, by her somewhat stiff attitude and by the austere black of the sumptuous dress from Worth. The pastel colors of the identical dresses of Georgette and Paul – who is also dressed as a girl, according to the custom of the day for small boys – provide a touch of tenderness to offset the severity. However, if Madame Charpentier is striking a pose, the children are quite natural. The exchange of glances and the position of the girl sitting on the dog's back bring a note of freshness to this sophisticated work. We also perceive a touch of humor when we notice the parallel between the black and white fur of the

St. Bernard and the outfit of the lady of the house. The portrait of this protectress of the arts and letters, hung to such advantage at the show, was received with all due respect. Even someone as hostile to Renoir as Arthur Baignières wrote in the *Gazette des Beaux-Arts* : "Let us not quarrel with Monsieur Renoir; he has returned to the bosom of the Church; let us welcome his return, forget about form and speak only of coloring." And Charles Tardieu added in *L'Art*: "Impressionism? It has cleaned itself up, it has put on gloves. Soon it will be dining out in town." Later Renoir thrust back at all those who were dinning the phrase "his supreme masterpiece" into his ears: "Put it in the Louvre and leave it in peace."

JEANNE SAMARY, 1878
Oil on canvas, 173 x 102 cm
*The Hermitage Museum,
St. Petersburg*

JEANNE SAMARY

Her beauty, charm, and
success made this actress
the toast of the fashionable
salons. First prize at the
Conservatoire in 1874,
the piquante, red-haired
Jeanne made her debut
in 1875 at the Comédie-
Française and became a
member in 1879. She
triumphed in *A Boring
World*, a play by Édouard
Pailleron. Renoir, who
loved to draw inspiration
from budding actresses,
often saw her
in Montmartre and in
Madame Charpentier's
drawing room. As early as
the third, Impressionist
exhibition in 1877, his bust
of the actress had attracted
attention. An enthusiastic
critic, Philippe Burty, even
evoked Fragonard when
speaking of it.
In the picture in the
Hermitage Museum, the
emphasis is on the clothes,
the hair, and the
expression of the eyes; the
rest is just accessory.
Closed to the left by a
panel decorated in Chinese
style, the background
opens onto a zone of
shadow lit by the dim glow
of a copper flowerpot. A
simple layout (2/3, 1/3)
divides the space across. It
is not exactly respected in
height, which gives the
carpet a kind of verticality
which projects the
silhouette of the actress
towards the front. She is
not blended into
the atmosphere by the
Impressionist technique of
a myriad of brush strokes;
she stands out without
transition from the flecks
on the floor and the

penumbra of the room behind.

Like the Venetians (Veronese, Tintoretto), the painter takes delight in detailing the fabrics, playing a whole rainbow of variegated patterns on the white satin and Chantilly lace. This is a ball gown of the kind that his friend Mallarmé described in *La Nouvelle Mode* : "...bodice and skirt mould the figure more than ever; delicious contrast between vagueness and what has to be accentuated." Renoir almost failed to finish the picture, exasperated by the repeated failure of the young woman to turn up for the posing sessions they had arranged. However, he managed to communicate an intense feeling of life to this beautiful Samary, who seems to be acknowledging the applause of her audience after the last act of a play at the Théâtre-Français. Hung at the Salon in 1879, the portrait was badly placed, no doubt so as not to overshadow *Madame Charpentier and Her Children*. Outraged by that hanging of a picture which had so delighted him, the writer Joris-Karl Huysmans exclaimed: "They might as well hang the paintings along the ceiling while they're about it."

We shall be seeing the actress again in *The Luncheon of the Boating Party*. She died in 1890, at the age of 33, of typhoid fever. "What a charming girl," Renoir recalled twenty years later, "and what a skin! She positively lit up everything around her."

In close up, slightly to the right of the composition, the young woman has her back to the river, on which a boat is sailing away. All the colors of the spectrum, taken up in a light range which the color of trees in springtime, intermingle in small strokes to evoke the willows below the terrace and the thick foliage on the opposite bank. By means of the play of reflections, the dress becomes opaline and part of the almost palpable impression of diffuse light and moisture. The yellow straw of the hat shadows the hair with russet and the red ribbon enlivens the set of pale harmonies.

In *Paul's Wife* Guy de Maupassant describes this place, which was one of his haunts, under the name of the "Restaurant Grillon". The novelist, a member of the Naturalist

ALPHONSINE FOURNAISE, 1879
Oil on canvas, 73 x 93 cm
Musée d'Orsay, Paris

ALPHONSINE FOURNAISE

On the banks of the Seine, on the Île de Chatou, the Fournaise Inn (now a restaurant and museum) was one of the fashionable spots where boating parties rubbed shoulders with leading figures of the theatre and literature. In this portrait – for a long time given the incorrect title of *À la*

Grenouillère – of the restaurant owner's daughter, Alphonsine, Renoir is trying not so much to define the model and the place as to prove to what extent atmosphere can modify a character.

movement, evokes "the tall young men in their white vests" and "the women in light-colored spring dresses" who meet at this "boatmen's hangout".

Renoir shows Alphonsine with her elbow on a table, which is set in readiness for the customer. She seems to be following a carefree train of thought as she awaits the moment when, before her admirers, "she will dive like a champion swimmer to bring back from the bed of the river the golden louis that people throw for her." In the distance the Seine and the railway bridge are hazy in the most Impressionist of mists.

OARSMEN AT CHATOU, 1879
Oil on canvas, 81 x 100 cm
*National Gallery of Art (Gift of
Sam A. Lewisohn), Washington*

OARSMEN AT CHATOU

Boating is in fashion.
Crowds of people flock
happily in summer from
Paris to Chatou, Bougival
or Asnières. This is one of
Renoir's favorite themes,
as it provides him with an
opportunity to paint
figures and landscapes at
the same time.
In this composition, the
river bank at Rueil closes
the background
horizontally; the Chatou
side, in the foreground,
follows a diagonal which
gives the Seine an effect of
breadth and the slow
gliding of the current.
The oblique line of the
skiff separates the land
where the people are
standing from the
plane of the water.
The effect of perspective

is created by different
values: dark in the
foreground of the picture,
medium in the line of the
houses and the troubled
sky, very light on the
surface in the medium
ground, where the
shimmer of the water
draws the eye towards the
center of the picture. The
touches of cerulean blue
and white are enlivened
with pinks, violets, and
crimsons, tinged with
orange beneath the
mahogany of the boat.
Different elements of river
life are set side by side:
two skiffs are being rowed
by, there is a barge
alongside the towpath, a
sailing boat is tacking
round the bend.
It is not the faces, which
are barely sketched in,
which have attracted the

painter's attention, but the clothes and the movements of the people. Each is dressed according to his part: blue trousers, red sash, and straw boater for the young oarsman, brown jersey for the old sailor, white jacket and scarlet riding coat for the Parisians on an outing. Everything suggests the imminence of departure: the man hiring the boat is getting ready to push out the skiff with its elegant occupants: Aline Charigot, the future Madame Renoir, is gathering up her skirt, revealing the lace flounces, while her companion is getting ready to follow her; Franc-Lamy is grasping an oar and turning to greet his passengers. The very elements take part in the general animation: the reeds bending on the river bank, the ripples on the water, the clouds scudding across the sky.

Water, clouds, wind, the pleasure of an outing on the Seine, all the components of the Impressionist universe are here in this work which, with its theme and tonality, already foreshadows *The Luncheon of the Boating Party* which Renoir was to begin the following year on the same Île de Chatou.

THE LUNCHEON OF THE BOATING PARTY, 1880-1881
Oil on canvas, 130 x 173 cm
The Phillips Collection, Washington

THE LUNCHEON OF THE BOATING PARTY

When he started this picture, in the summer of 1880, Renoir was well aware of the ambitious scope of his project. He wrote to Bérard: "I am at Chatou... I am doing a picture of boatmen which has been gnawing at me for some time... From time to time you need to try something which is beyond your powers." And, indeed, the Fournaise Restaurant, with its festive atmosphere, its tumult of noise and color, inspired Renoir to paint one of the great Impressionist canvases. It evokes a memory, though adapted to the profane world, of one of the painter's favorite works, *The Wedding at Cana* by Veronese, which he had himself taken to see in the last year of his life. Here the atmosphere of popular gaiety is similar to *Dance at the Moulin de la Galette*, but in five years the treatment has changed. True, Renoir, according to his custom, represents friends, the regulars at the inn, but he does not sink them into the atmosphere with a thousand dazzling strokes; he rediscovers a certain respect for local tone.
His composition is ordered along two diagonals. One joins the men in their vests, the archetypes of the boatman. The other leads from the left-hand side of the tablecloth to the upper right-hand background, creating an effect of depth. At the point of intersection is the shining lunch table, the reason for this meeting of different people and a picture within the picture. On its iridescent whites the carefully arranged disorder

of the table shows the end of a meal washed down with plenty of wine. A remarkable chromatism brings together the mahogany of the barrel, the green of the bottles, and the purple of their contents and subtly distinguishes the red of the wine, the black of the coffee, and the amber of the liqueurs. A ray of sun lights up Aline Charigot, Renoir's latest woman friend, all freshness and sensuality with her hat decorated with poppies, whose scarlet echoes the red of the awning which bathes the terrace in warm tones. A humorous note is struck by placing her pug profile face to face with the muzzle of the little terrier. Behind her Fournaise junior, striking an advantageous pose, surveys his customers. Leaning on the verandah, his sister Alphonsine is listening with an air of false candor to Baron Barbier. His back marks the border between the leading figures of the picture and the friendly supporting cast. In front, Aline's natural manner is in contrast with the sophistication of the young woman on the right, the elegant actress Ellen Andrée who, beneath the slightly jealous gaze of the journalist Maggiolo, is playing a seduction scene with her young neighbor. Behind, there is a hint of haze about the woman drinking (Angèle), the man in the top hat (the financier Ephrussi) and Lestringuez and Lhote, who are joking with Jeanne Samary. Only the landscape is executed with a completely Impressionist technique in the dancing shadows of the willows and the shimmer of the river, where light boats are sailing. Surrounded by the framework of greenery, the different groups blend into the atmosphere of gaiety which gives unity to the scene. *La Grenouillère, Dance at the Moulin de la Galette, The Luncheon of the Boating Party*; Renoir is indeed the painter of the "fêtes galantes" of his century.

THE UMBRELLAS, 1881-1885
Oil on canvas, 180 x 115 cm
The National Gallery, London

THE UMBRELLAS

The movement of this crowd has nothing to do with the movements of the people in *Dance at the Moulin de la Galette* or *The Luncheon of the Boating Party*. The composition, sharp and precise, plays rather on the forms – the circles or semicircles of the hoop, the umbrellas, the basket – than on the deliberately bluish play of light and shadow. This work dates from a period of transition, when Renoir, a prey to doubt, was searching for a new style.

It is imbued with that Japanese style that was all the rage at the time in Parisian artistic circles. The influence of Hokusai and his rain scenes is evident here. The canvas is also close to an engraving done by Manet during the war, *The Queue at the Butcher's Shop*; a nod or a tribute to the master who died in 1883?

Might *The Umbrellas* have been painted during two

different periods? The dichotomy of the canvas leads us to think so. The right-hand part, where the elegant woman and the children are treated with small, discontinuous touches and their features suggested rather than defined, could have been painted in early 1881. The woman with the basket (on the left), on the other hand, is clearly outlined and might date from 1883-1885. Her well drawn silhouette and her more dryly classical treatment herald the period known as "hard". Renoir's brother, Edmond, and their friend Paul Lhote were the inspiration for the man who is captivated by the charms of the young laundress. The model was Suzanne Valadon, who was later to become famous as a painter. A social connotation, a rare event with Renoir, appears in the juxtaposition of the two female figures: on the one side, the bourgeoise with her eyes lowered, and on the other the "bareheaded" woman, dressed in the gray worker's uniform.

DANCE IN THE CITY,
1882-1883
Oil on canvas, 180 x 90 cm
Musée d'Orsay, Paris

DANCE IN THE CITY

At the major Renoir
retrospective in 1883, at
Durand-Ruel's gallery, his
three latest pictures (dance
scenes) caught the eye of
Paris shortly before being
shown, the same year, in
London. Two of them,
done in the same format
– one symbolizing
the city, the other the
country – are intended to
be hung side by side. The
third, *Dance at Bougival*
(Boston Museum), seems
to be designed to be sold
independently. The dancer
in the three canvases is
Paul Lhote, one of
Renoir's best friends, who
went with him to Algeria,
Italy, and the Channel
Islands. The former naval
officer, who worked for
the Havas Agency, an art
lover and something of an
amateur painter himself,
often appears in Renoir's
pictures. A peculiarity of
his: he regularly fell in
love with his friend's
models.
And it would be hard to
remain indifferent to the
charms of his partner,
Marie-Clémentine, the
future Suzanne Valadon
and mother of Maurice
Utrillo. The seventeen-
year-old laundress posed
at the time for artists, from
Puvis de Chavannes to
Degas and Toulouse-
Lautrec. "How many
poses I have done for
Renoir," she told her first
biographers, "whether in
the studio in the Rue
Saint-Georges or the one

in the Rue d'Orchampt."
We also find her in
The Braid (1884), the
masterpiece of the
Ingres period.
The position of the bodies
in *Dance in the City*
indicates that they are
dancing a waltz, the only
dance at that time where
the couple were so close to
each other. In this
depthless composition, the
gentleman's black coat
and the young girl's glove
isolate the pair linearly
from the indistinct mass of
palms and lilac. This
precise line already
heralds the style of the

hard period. The orange
color of the floor
complements the
background greenery.
The whiteness of the
dress reflects the
iridescence which is
echoed, in the
background, by the
imitation marble of
the column.
The sobriety of
the picture recalls the
portraits (like the one
of Valtesse de la Bigne,
1879) which made the
success of his friend
Gervex, one of the
characters in *Dance at the
Moulin de la Galette*.

Dance in the City breathes
elegance and distinction:
the soberly drawn floral
composition, the
restrained movement of
the arms, the sobriety
of the hairstyle. Unlike
Dance in the Country,
there is no sense of letting
go. With this couple, the
man is just a silhouette
and the young girl
symbolizes all the
refinement of Paris
fashion embodied in the
dress so voluptuously
draped by the painter's
hand. The sole ornament,
the rose in her hair, could
be Renoir's signature.

DANCE IN THE COUNTRY,
1882-1883
Oil on canvas, 180 x 90 cm
Musée d'Orsay, Paris

DANCE IN THE COUNTRY

The elegance and restraint of *Dance in the City* is in contrast to the joyfully relaxed attitude of the couple in the country. Once again we have Paul Lhote and, this time, Aline Charigot. Who better than the painter's woman friend from Champagne to symbolize the unaffected charm of this country ball? With the freshness of her twenty years, her curves so dear to Renoir and her talent for the waltz, she is the very embodiment of the simple delights provided by the pleasure gardens the painter loved so much.

The composition is apparently identical to that of *Dance in the City*: a couple in dark suit and light colored dress are dancing in each other's arms. But everything is different. The decorative frame has changed its nature. The banal foliage of a chestnut tree replaces the subtle floral arrangement. The bare stucco of the ballroom depicted in *Dance in the City* gives way to objects presented in a certain disorder: a cheap fan and the table which, with its crumpled cloth and the spoon standing in the cup, awaits the return of the dancers.

Moreover, the very function of the decor – here the terrace of Fournaise – has changed. Instead of being isolated in a timeless world, the couple in *Dance in the Country* are not abstracted from their immediate surroundings. The straw hat which has rolled into the foreground

suggests a recent stroll. It also serves to hold the eye and, like the faces above it, to give the impression of a succession of planes to this composition which is deliberately more stripped of depth than the beautiful drawing which preceded it (graphic arts department, Louvre Museum).

Another difference between the two dances is the general tonality. The coldness of the black and white palette of the one is contrasted with the warm tones of the other. The navy blue worn by Paul Lhote highlights the dress with the roses, whose red madder is echoed in the outlandish bonnet.

As it should, the rustic linen which brings out Aline's curves breaks with the damask satin of *Dance in the City*. And Paul, on this outing to the country, is not wearing gloves. The positions of the bodies are also different: the attitudes of the couple reveal Paul's contained desire and Aline's face radiant with pleasure. Her gaze is not directed at her partner, but at the painter who is immortalizing the moment. A moment of abandonment when Aline, wild with happiness and fatigue, lets herself sink onto her partner's shoulder. That joy of living, that atmosphere of a bygone age, was revived by the painter's son, the director Jean Renoir, in a famous film, *La Partie de campagne*.

THE CHILDREN'S AFTERNOON
AT WARGEMONT, 1884
Oil on canvas, 127 x 173 cm
*Nationalgalerie, Staatliche
Museen, Berlin*

THE CHILDREN'S AFTERNOON AT WARGEMONT

On several occasions during the 1880s, Renoir was Paul Bérard's guest at the Château de Wargemont on the coast of Normandy. In two years he painted thirteen portraits for the great art lover, among them *Marthe, Little Girl with a Blue Sash* (São Paulo Museum), *Lucie* (Art Institute, Chicago) and *Margot* (Metropolitan Museum). This large format painting, Bérard's most important commission, is the masterpiece of the so-called "Ingres" or "hard" style, which was to culminate, though less happily, in the large *Bathers* which is now in the Philadelphia Museum. The brush is precise, the lines firm and the use of Impressionist touches is limited to the evocation of the landscape, symbolized by rapid diagonals of green and chrome yellow. The picture is once again an abstract surface which receives all the geometrical motifs present in the room: the rectangles of the windows and the woodwork, the diagonals of the parquet, the stripes of the sofa, the chequers of a skirt, the dots on a dress, the triangle of a sailor top, even down to the skilful ornamentation of the cloth on the table discreetly signed in one corner by the painter. Renoir was attempting to compete with himself by using a new manner in a large group portrait which can be set alongside the one of *Madame Charpentier*. While painting that, he had Ingres' *Madame Rivière* in mind. At Wargemont, he was inspired by the smooth lineal grace of *Mademoiselle Rivière*. The light tones of the whole painting are divided into two different parts, according to the golden mean: on the left a play of cold, limpid blues, and on the right warm colors. The crimsons of the sash, the curtains or the table, the brighter vermilion of the begonias warm the slightly austere atmosphere of the piece. The girls on the right are contained in an invisible circle which circumscribes the action. The eldest is sewing a dress for the youngest one's doll, thus occupying her attention while she poses. On the left the fair hair lights up a dazzling range of blues. The off-center composition makes the scene more intimate. The air of application of Marthe bending over her work, the thoughtful gaze of little Lucie and the serious attitude of Marguerite, isolated in the reading of her album, illustrate a moment of respite from the bustle of a children's afternoon. Everything breathes the limpid serenity of a day on holiday. The only movements are those of the hands using the needle and the discreet ballet of the shoes which each have their own individuality. This interior recalls the Dutch paintings of the 17th century, but it also evokes, in its pared down simplicity, the frescoes of the Quattrocento or the Raphaels that Renoir had just been admiring in Italy.

**YOUNG GIRLS
AT THE PIANO,** 1892
Oil on canvas, 116 x 90 cm
Musée d'Orsay, Paris

YOUNG GIRLS AT THE PIANO

Thanks to these delightful
girls, at the age of 51
Renoir became the first
Impressionist to be
admitted to the
Luxembourg, the modern
art museum of the day.
The picture was not
acquired at an exhibition,
but bought for the nation
by the director of the
Beaux-Arts, Henri Roujon,
on the recommendation of
Stéphane Mallarmé.
Music had always played
an important part in the
artist's life. Among his
best friends were a number
of music lovers – Bazille,
Edmond Maître –, the
Bohemian musician
Cabaner and the
composers Gabriel Fauré,
Jacques Offenbach, and
Emmanuel Chabrier.
The painter had already
treated this classic theme
in 1876, the date of
Woman at the Piano, done
in a purely Impressionist
style. In 1888 he
represented in his Ingres
manner *Catulle Mendès'
Daughters at Their Piano*,
and then, in 1889, *The
Piano Lesson* – which,
like this *Young Girls at the
Piano*, was shown at the
great retrospective
in 1892 – and, in 1897,
the daughters of the
painter Henri Lerolle, a
friend of Claude Debussy.
This picture dates for the
time when Renoir,
distancing himself from
the "hard" period,
tackled the "mother-of-

pearl" style, renewing his links with a light Impressionism, with gentle undertones. No aggressive colors, not the slightest sharp line. The keynote of the canvas is harmony: the harmony of colors where the painter plays on subtle variations of orange mixed with greens and yellows, where fragile pinks brush against pearly whites, barely heightened with pearl blue, where the bouquet subdues its burst of color and the piano is almost blond. Harmony too in the composition, which rests first and foremost on the curves of the objects (vase, piano, curtains) and the girls (two sisters); the closeness of their heads and the position of their bodies indicate intimacy, while their graceful movements are stamped with a certain slowness. And harmony in the faces with their tangerine tinge which, beneath the different colors of their hair – one fair, the other chestnut – are alike and at one in the shared pleasure of music.

There is also a strong impression of fluidity, very typical of the period, in this scene: the soft movement of the curtain, revealing the intimacy of a bedroom in the background, the ill-defined contours of the dresses, the cascade of hair prolonged by an untied sash.

Is this *Young Girls at the Piano* hanging in the Luxembourg the best of the five or six versions presented to the nation by Renoir? Not if we are to believe the artist himself who, always hesitant, was later to show a clear preference for the one dedicated to his friend Caillebotte.

BATHER ARRANGING HER HAIR, 1893
Oil on canvas, 92 x 74 cm
National Gallery of Art (Chester Dale Collection), Washington

BATHER ARRANGING HER HAIR

Since the 18th century, women bathing had been the classic expression of the nude. Renoir was an admirer of Boucher and Fragonard and his career abounds in versions of this motif. The realism of *Bather with Terrier* (1870) evolves into pure Impressionism in *After the Bath* (1876) and the canvases posed for by Anna, the model for *Torso in the Sun. Blonde Bather* (1881), a transitional work, heralds the large canvas of *Bathers* (1887), the apogee of the Ingres style. *Bather Arranging Her Hair* belongs to the period known as "mother-of-pearl", which was to be followed by a series of nudes in the manner of Rubens.

After 1888, obeying the dictates of his innermost temperament, Renoir painted a large number of women bathing, at rest, like iridescent shells, against rainbow backgrounds. Slumbering or daydreaming, sitting on rocks, playing with their flowing hair, frolicking with their companions, they are sometimes very young girls, sometimes grown women.

In 1893 Renoir spent the month of August at Pont-Aven. The shady background opening onto

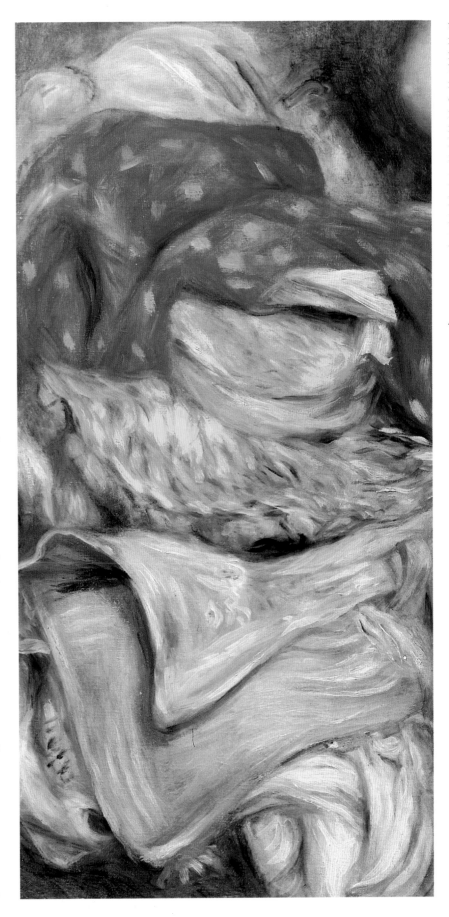

the sunlit rocks is a memory of the Breton forest. The composition brings the torso and belly into prominence at the expense of the face, flushed with heat but relegated to the shadows. It also gives considerable importance to the accumulation of fabrics whose scarlets and pinks highlight the mother-of-pearl of the skin. The pure lines of the silhouette – the triangle formed by the arms, the roundness of the breasts, the curve of the hip – and the smooth nudity are opposed to the jumble of clothes, carelessly heaped up in layers. The choice of pose (arms raised) emphasises the bust: the breasts are erect, the waist is arched. As always, Renoir gives primacy to the natural. This is no longer an adolescent with long flowing hair, but a woman pinning it up before putting on her garments, cast aside in haste before bathing. We find the accessories that appear in various nudes: the large straw hat, symbol of an eternal summer, the linen rumpled around the thighs, to reveal or conceal one intimate part or another at the whim of the composition.

The redcurrant dress with white spots is the one worn in several paintings by one of the sisters who posed frequently for Berthe Morisot and Renoir. Renoir celebrates the female body in a joy which has no place for vice. To represent "the skin of a young girl," that is the height of happiness for the painter who had always considered the nude as "one of the indispensable art forms."

GABRIELLE AND JEAN, 1895
Oil on canvas, 65 x 54 cm
Musée de l'Orangerie (Walter-Guillaume Collection), Paris

GABRIELLE AND JEAN

Renoir never tired of painting his children. Pierre (1885-1952), who became a famous actor, Jean (1894-1979), the future film director, and Claude (1901-1969), the ceramicist whose birth acted as a spur to Renoir's creation when he had fallen into a declining state of health. He represented them all at different stages of childhood, from the baby suckled

by his mother (*Motherhood*, 1886) to the small boy studying his lessons or reading (*Lunch at Berneval*, 1898, *Coco's Writing Lesson*, 1906-1907).

Beside them, almost always, was Gabrielle Renard. She was 15 when she arrived in Montmartre, at the Château des Brouillards. This cousin of Madame Renoir, from Essoyes like her, came to help her run her household when Jean was born. She stayed until 1914, filling the roles of servant, big sister, and then model. She was famous for her blunders at the time. The faces of Gabrielle and Jean radiate health and happiness, a reflection of that intimate joy which Renoir loved to paint. He also found in the young girl that Venusian beauty that so charmed him. As Jean Renoir says in his *Souvenirs* about the actress Jeanne Samary: "Above all she was a Renoir. She belongs to that immense family that goes from my mother to Nini by way of the Bérard children, Gabrielle, Suzanne Valadon and us, the Renoir children. We are all alike."

**DANCER
WITH CASTANETS,** 1909
Oil on canvas, 155 x 65 cm
The National Gallery, London

DANCER WITH CASTANETS

In the last ten years of his life Renoir, increasingly handicapped by acute multiple arthritis, painted hardly any more large format works, still less decorative panels like the ones he had done for the Charpentiers or Dr Blanche. This *Dancer with Castanets* and its companion piece, *Dancer with Tambourine*, are the exceptions. They can be attributed to his friendship with the collector Maurice Gangnat, who commissioned them for his drawing-room.

The painter had just moved into his house at Les Collettes, where the largest of the three studios planned by his architect was ideally suited to this kind of work. Castanets and tambourine are allusions to his visit to Spain in 1892 with Paul Gallimard. If the austerity of the Iberian landscapes had been ill-suited to his taste for a luxuriant, colorful nature, he was nonetheless fired with enthusiasm for the regional costumes and the sequined suits of the bullfighters. A few years later, that interest was echoed by his portrait of *Ambroise Vollard in Toreador's Costume.*

plenitude and the bursts which emphasize it, the color does not make the picture and this composition by masses seems close to sculpture. The fact of having entertained Maillol at Essoyes the previous summer is surely not unconnected with this new vision of the artist.
The whole rhythm is conveyed through simple

The *Dancer with Castanets* is typical of the period when Renoir was devoting his final strength to the evocation of the female body. While in the dances *In the City*, *In the Country* and *At Bougival* the attention is held by a certain symbolism, here the cynosure is undoubtedly the opulent forms of the model. The garlands of sequins and roses follow the curves of the body. The hair soberly held back by a crown of flowers reveals the ear with its shining pearl. A necklace emphasizes the roundness of the neck and follows the movement of the bodice, covered by a glittering bolero jacket. The costume looks less Spanish than Oriental, as witness the sash tied below the hips and the embroidered slippers. Although it is covered, the body is no less apparent beneath the shimmering flow of the fabric and seems to be moving in a slow undulation, the kind to be seen in the belly dance. In spite of its

gestures: the graceful circle formed by the right arm is answered by the bend of the left, which brings out the line of the neck and shoulders. While the body seems to be offering itself to the public, the face is looking inwards. The lowered eyes, the introverted air; the young woman with the castanets belongs only to the dance.

GABRIELLE WITH ROSE, 1911
Oil on canvas, 55 x 47 cm
Musée d'Orsay, Paris

GABRIELLE WITH ROSE

Servant and model,
Gabrielle Renard reigned
over Renoir's last creative
years. She left in 1914,
doubtless after falling out
with Madame Renoir, and
became the wife of the
American painter
Conrad Slade.
This sensual, petulant and
"natural" brunette
delighted the man she
affectionately called "the
boss". Anyone who
wanted to approach the
painter, who was then at
the height of his glory,
had to reckon with her
unpredictable
temperament. Between
1907 and 1910 she
inspired portraits, nudes,
bathers and even male
characters, such as the
shepherd Paris in *The
Judgement of Paris*
(1914), for which she
posed with Marie,
nicknamed "the baker's
wife". In the evening of
his life, female forms were
one of the main sources of
inspiration for the painter,
who used models from his
own entourage, servants
or young women from
Essoyes and Cagnes.
In this last period, the
artist, confined to his
armchair, his fingers
misshapen with arthritis,
lived through a hell of

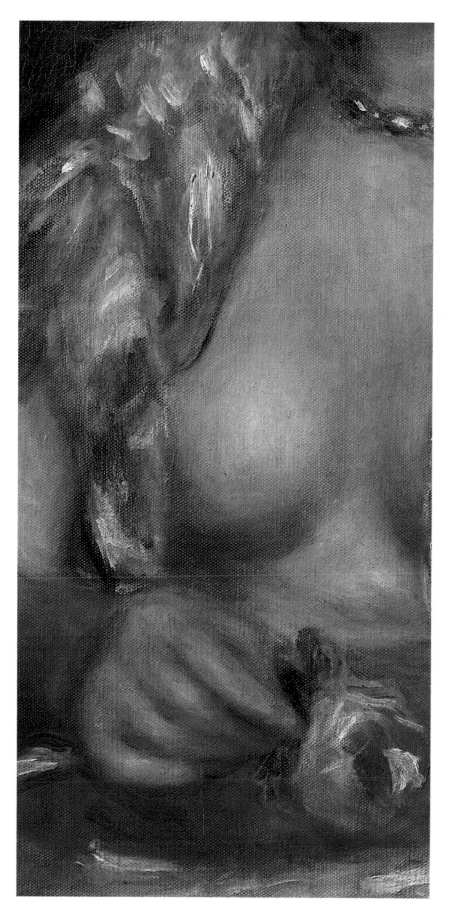

suffering. But what
mastery in this canvas on a
theme – a woman at her
toilet – which was rather
unusual for Renoir. The
harmony of red and green
reminds us of Delacroix.
The complexion of this
young woman adorning
herself is heightened with
carmine. The rose she is
holding close to her face
alludes to her burgeoning
freshness. Having
observed that colors faded
with time, the artist
accentuated them:
"I want," he wrote, "a red
to ring out like a bell and
if it does not I add color
until it does."

**BATHER DRYING
HER LEG,** c. 1910-1911
Oil on canvas, 84 x 65 cm
Museu de Arte, São Paulo

BATHER DRYING HER LEG

The more Renoir felt physically diminished, the more he celebrated the female body in all its fullness. A sort of frenzy and jubilation are mingled with the voluptuousness of still being able to paint, in spite of everything. The critic Félix Fénéon saw him as "an old pagan shepherd leading his troupe of goddesses towards the pond and the pasture: there they are frolicking, bathing, drying themselves, dozing, stretched out, pearly or reddish, massive, fleshy, blooming."

The delicate colored lightness of the mother-of-pearl period was followed by a style in the order of Rubens. The year before, while looking at one of his paintings in Munich, Renoir had exclaimed: "Here is the most radiant fullness, the most beautiful color. But the paint is very thin." On his return his bathers became more voluptuous and occupied, like the one here, practically the whole space. Perhaps we should also see here the influence of Cézanne's investigations into volumes.

The background is no longer, as in the previous period, a paradise of mother-of-pearl and blue. It is barely suggested by the small touches of woven colors that

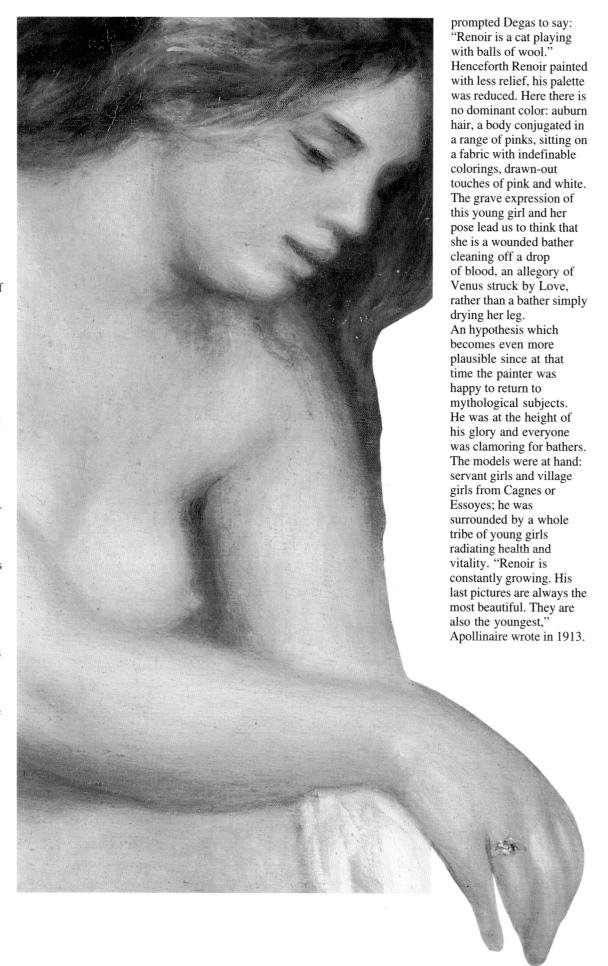

prompted Degas to say: "Renoir is a cat playing with balls of wool." Henceforth Renoir painted with less relief, his palette was reduced. Here there is no dominant color: auburn hair, a body conjugated in a range of pinks, sitting on a fabric with indefinable colorings, drawn-out touches of pink and white. The grave expression of this young girl and her pose lead us to think that she is a wounded bather cleaning off a drop of blood, an allegory of Venus struck by Love, rather than a bather simply drying her leg.

An hypothesis which becomes even more plausible since at that time the painter was happy to return to mythological subjects. He was at the height of his glory and everyone was clamoring for bathers. The models were at hand: servant girls and village girls from Cagnes or Essoyes; he was surrounded by a whole tribe of young girls radiating health and vitality. "Renoir is constantly growing. His last pictures are always the most beautiful. They are also the youngest," Apollinaire wrote in 1913.

Renoir

The Complete Works

WORKS

1 • Portrait of Renoir's Mother (Marguerite Merlet), 1860
Oil on canvas, 45 x 38 cm
Private Collection

2 • Pierrot and Colombine, 1861
Oil on canvas, 28 x 23 cm
Private Collection

3 • Bather Sleeping, 1861
Oil on canvas, 41 x 33 cm
Narodni muzej, Belgrade

4 • Émile-Henri Laporte, 1864
Oil on canvas, 55 x 46 cm
Private Collection

5 • William Sisley, 1864
Oil on canvas, 81 x 66 cm
Musée d'Orsay, Paris

6 • Mademoiselle Romaine Lacaux, 1864
Oil on canvas, 81 x 65 cm
The Museum of Art, Cleveland

7 • Still Life with Arums and Flowers, 1864
Oil on canvas, 130 x 96 cm
Oskar Reinhart Foundation, Winterthur

8 • Still Life, 1864
Oil on canvas, 35 x 46 cm
Kunsthalle, Hamburg

9 • La Clairière, 1865
Oil on canvas, 54 x 81 cm
Private Collection

10 • Trees in the Forest, 1866
Oil on canvas, 73 x 60 cm
Private Collection

11 • Jules Le Cœur in the Forest of Fontainebleau, 1866
Oil on canvas, 106 x 80 cm
Museu de Arte, São Paulo

12 • Vase of Flowers, 1866
Oil on canvas, 104 x 80 cm
The Fogg Art Museum, Cambridge (Massachusetts)

13 • Lise Sewing, 1866
Oil on canvas, 56 x 47 cm
Reves Collection, Roquebrune

14 • Le Cabaret de la Mère Antony, 1866
Oil on canvas, 195 x 130 cm
Nationalmuseum, Stockholm

15 • Madame Joseph Le Cœur, 1866
Oil on canvas, 116 x 87 cm
Musée d'Orsay, Paris

16 • Woman with Bird, 1866
Oil on canvas, 81 x 65 cm
Baron of Herzog Collection, Budapest

1 2 3
4 5
6 7 8
9 10
11 12 13
14 15 16

17 • Portrait of Lise, 1866
Oil on canvas, 46 x 37 cm
The Barnes Foundation, Merion

**18 • Bazille Painting at
His Easel, 1867**
Oil on canvas, 105 x 73 cm
Musée d'Orsay, Paris

**19 • The Champs-Elysées during the
Universal Exhibition of 1867**
Oil on canvas, 76.5 x 13 cm
Wildenstein Collection, New York

20 • Diana, 1867
Oil on canvas, 197 x 132 cm
National Gallery of Art, Washington

**21 • Lise with a Bunch of
Wildflowers, 1867**
Oil on canvas, 65 x 50 cm
Private Collection

22 • Lise with Sunshade, 1867
Oil on canvas, 184 x 115 cm
Museum Folkwang, Essen

23 • The Pont des Arts, 1867
Oil on canvas, 62 x 103 cm
Norton Simon Foundation, Pasadena

24 • Portrait of Alfred Sisley, 1868
Oil on canvas, 81 x 65 cm
Bührle Collection, Zurich

25 • The Clown, 1868
Oil on canvas, 192 x 128 cm
Rijksmuseum Kröller-Müller, Otterlo

**26 • Skaters in the Bois de
Boulogne, 1868**
Oil on canvas, 72 x 92 cm
Private Collection

27 • Boy with Cat, 1868
Oil on canvas, 124 x 67 cm
Musée d'Orsay, Paris

**28 • Summer, also called Lise or La
Bohémienne, 1868**
Oil on canvas, 85 x 59 cm
*Nationalgalerie, Staatliche Museen,
Berlin*

29 • Still Life with Roses, c. 1868
Oil on canvas, 72 x 53 cm
*The Fogg Art Museum, Cambridge
(Massachusetts)*

30 • Woman in a Garden, c. 1868
Oil on canvas, 106 x 73 cm
*Private Collection (on loan to
Kunstmuseum, Basel)*

**31 • Alfred Sisley and His Wife,
c. 1868**
Oil on canvas, 105 x 75 cm
Wallraf-Richartz Museum, Cologne

**32 • Still Life with Partridge,
1868-1870**
Oil on canvas, 33 x 40 cm
Private Collection

WORKS

33 • Bathing on the Seine, La Grenouillère, 1869
Oil on canvas, 59 x 80 cm
Pushkin Museum, Moscow

34 • La Grenouillère, 1869
Oil on canvas, 66 x 86 cm
Nationalmuseum, Stockholm

35 • The Grenouillère, 1869
Oil on canvas, 65 x 93 cm
Oskar Reinhart Foundation, Winterthur

36 • Boat in Chatou, 1869
Oil on canvas, 25 x 34 cm
Private Collection

37 • The Nymph at the Spring, 1869
Oil on canvas, 66 x 124 cm
The National Gallery, London

38 • Portrait of the Artist's Father, 1869
Oil on canvas, 61 x 48 cm
The Art Museum, St Louis

39 • Woman with Lace Bodice, 1869
Oil on canvas, 81 x 65 cm
Private Collection

40 • La Grenouillère, 1869
Oil on canvas, 50 x 57 cm
Private Collection

41 • Barges on the Seine, c. 1869
Oil on canvas, 47 x 64 cm
Musée d'Orsay, Paris

42 • Flowers in a Vase, c. 1869
Oil on canvas, 65 x 54 cm
Museum of Fine Arts, Boston

43 • Madame Théodore Charpentier, c. 1869
Oil on canvas, 46 x 64 cm
Musée d'Orsay, Paris

44 • The English Pear Tree, c. 1869-1870
Oil on canvas, 64 x 81 cm
Private Collection

45 • View of Louveciennes, 1870
Oil on canvas, 33 x 41 cm
Private Collection

46 • Young Girl at Her Window, 1870
Oil on canvas, 55 x 46 cm
Private Collection

47 • Portrait of Marie Le Cœur, 1870
Oil on canvas, 41 x 33 cm
Musée des Beaux-Arts, Strasbourg

33

34

35

36

37

38

39

40

41

42

43

44

45

46

47

48
49
50
51
52
53
54
55
56
57
58
59
60
61
62
63
64

48 • Young Girl in a Boat, 1870
Oil on canvas, 18 x 27 cm
Private Collection

49 • Young Woman in a Boat, 1870
Oil on canvas, 26 x 32 cm
Private Collection

50 • Woman on the Banks of the Water, 1870
Oil on canvas, 16 x 26 cm
Private Collection

51 • Landscape with Woman, 1870
Oil on canvas, 25 x 15 cm
National Gallery of Art, Washington

52 • Bather with a Griffon (Bather with Terrier), 1870
Oil on canvas, 184 x 115 cm
Museu de Arte, São Paulo

53 • The Promenade, 1870
Oil on canvas, 80 x 64 cm
British Rail Pension Fund, London

54 • Woman of Algiers, 1870
Oil on canvas, 69 x 123 cm
National Gallery of Art, Washington

55 • Woman of Algiers, 1870
Oil on canvas, 84 x 60 cm
Museum of Modern Art, San Francisco

56 • Rapha Maître, 1870
Oil on canvas, 36 x 32 cm
Hausammann Collection, Zurich

57 • Pierre-Henri Renoir, 1870
Oil on canvas, 81 x 64 cm
Private Collection

58 • Portrait of Madame de Pourtalès (Mélanie de Pourtalès), 1870
Oil on canvas, 81 x 65 cm
The Fogg Art Museum, Cambridge (Massachusetts)

59 • Portrait of Madame Charles Le Cœur (Marie Charpentier), 1870
Oil on canvas, 25 x 19 cm
Private Collection

60 • Portrait of Charles Le Cœur, 1870
Oil on canvas, 25 x 19 cm
Private Collection

61 • Madame Massonie, c. 1870
Oil on canvas, 82 x 65 cm
Steinberg Collection, St Louis

62 • Field of Roses, 1870-1873
Oil on canvas, 38.5 x 46 cm
Private Collection

63 • Woman with Parrot, 1871
Oil on canvas, 91 x 65 cm
Thannhauser Fondation, New York

64 • Portrait of a Woman, Rapha, 1871
Oil on canvas, 130 x 83 cm
Private Collection

WORKS

65 • Portrait of Rapha Maître, 1871
Oil on canvas, 37 x 32 cm
Smith College Museum of Art,
Northampton

66 • Portrait of Edmond Maître
(The Reader), 1871
Oil on canvas, 21 x 28 cm
Private Collection

67 • Portrait of Madame
Darras, 1871
Oil on canvas, 81 x 65 cm
The Metropolitan Museum of Art, New
York

68 • Portrait of the Capitaine
Darras, 1871
Oil on canvas, 81 x 65 cm
Gemäldegalerie, Staatliche
Kunstsammlungen, Dresden

69 • Still Life with Bouquet of
Flowers, 1871
Oil on canvas, 74 x 59 cm
The Museum of Fine Arts, Houston

70 • Seine at Chatou, c. 1871
Oil on canvas, 46 x 61 cm
Art Gallery of Ontario, Toronto

71 • Portrait of Joseph Le Cœur,
1871-1872
Oil on canvas, 27 x 21 cm
Musée d'Unterlinden, Colmar

72 • The Rose, 1872
Oil on canvas, 29.5 x 25 cm
Musée d'Orsay, Paris

73 • Parisiennes en Algériennes, 1872
Oil on canvas, 156 x 129 cm
Museum of Western Art, Tokyo

74 • Woman with Parasol, 1872
Oil on canvas, 46 x 38 cm
Private Collection

75 • Young Girl with Parasol, 1872
Oil on canvas, 25 x 19 cm
Private Collection

76 • The Pont Neuf, Paris, 1872
Oil on canvas, 74 x 93 cm
National Gallery of Art, Washington

77 • The Meadow, 1872-1880 (?)
Oil on canvas, 32 x 46 cm

78 • Lise with Shawl, 1872
Oil on canvas, 56 x 47 cm
Reves Collection, Roquebrune

79 • Claude Monet Reading, 1872
Oil on canvas, 61 x 50 cm
Musée Marmottan, Paris

80 • Madame Claude Monet
Reading, 1872
Oil on canvas, 65 x 50 cm
Sterling and Francine Clark Art
Institute, Williamstown

65

66

67

68

69

70

71

72

73

74

75

76

77

78

79

80

81

82

83

84

85

86

87

88

89

90

91

92

93

94

95

96

**81 • Portrait of Claude Monet
(The Reader), 1872**
Oil on canvas, 61 x 50 cm
National Gallery of Art, Washington

**82 • Portrait of Madame
Monet, 1872**
Oil on canvas, 61 x 50 cm
Musée Marmottan, Paris

**83 • Woman Gathering
Flowers, 1872**
Oil on canvas, 65 x 54 cm
*Sterling and Francine Clark Art
Institute, Williamstown*

84 • Seated Nude, 1872
Oil on canvas, 38 x 25 cm
*Norton Simon Foundation, Los
Angeles*

**85 • The Fine Season
(The Conversation), 1872**
Oil on canvas, 60 x 33 cm
Private Collection

**86 • The Fine Season
(The Walk), 1872**
Oil on canvas, 44 x 20 cm
Private Collection

87 • Peonies in a Vase, 1872
Oil on canvas, 66 x 82 cm
Städtische Kunsthalle, Mannheim

88 • Vase of Flowers, 1872
Oil on canvas, 95 x 72 cm
Private Collection

89 • View of Conti Quay, 1872
Oil on canvas, 39 x 46 cm
Private Collection

**90 • Madame Monet Lying on a
Sofa, 1872**
Oil on canvas, 54 x 73 cm
*Calouste Gulbenkian Foundation,
Lisbon*

**91 • Still Life with Melon and Vase
of Flowers, 1872**
Oil on canvas, 54 x 65 cm
Private Collection

92 • The Gust of Wind, c. 1872
Oil on canvas, 52 x 82 cm
Fitzwilliam Museum, Cambridge

**93 • Portrait of Madame Monet,
1872-1875**
Oil on canvas, 36 x 32 cm
Peralta-Ramos Collection

94 • Oarsmen at Argenteuil, 1873
Oil on canvas, 50 x 61 cm
Private Collection

95 • The Watering Place, 1873
Oil on canvas, 46 x 61 cm
Private Collection

96 • The Harvesters, 1873
Oil on canvas, 60 x 73 cm
Bührle Collection, Zurich

WORKS

97 • Pool with Ducks, 1873
Oil on canvas, 49 x 60 cm
Valley House Gallery, Dallas

98 • Madame Darras, 1873
Oil on canvas, 47,5 x 39 cm
Musée d'Orsay, Paris

99 • Bridle Path in the Bois de Boulogne, 1873
Oil on canvas, 261 x 226 cm
Kunsthalle, Hamburg

100 • Woman in Garden, 1873
Oil on canvas, 65 x 54 cm
Private Collection

101 • Embroidering in the Park, 1873
Oil on canvas, 46 x 38 cm
Private Collection

102 • Portrait of a Man with Beard, 1873
Oil on canvas, 48 x 40 cm
Private Collection

103 • Bather Seated with Arms Raised, or Youth, c. 1873
Oil on canvas, 41 x 32 cm
Private Collection

104 • Young Woman in White Reading, 1873
Oil on canvas, 35 x 27 cm
Private Collection

105 • Woman with Parasol, 1873
Oil on canvas, 46 x 38 cm
Hughes Collection, New York

106 • Mademoiselle Marthe Le Cœur, 1873
Oil on canvas, 39 x 27 cm
Private Collection

107 • The Theatre Box, 1873
Oil on canvas, 27 x 21 cm
Private Collection

108 • Banks of the Seine at Argenteuil, 1873
Oil on canvas, 50 x 65 cm
Private Collection

109 • Monet Working in His Garden, 1873
Oil on canvas, 46 x 60 cm
Wadsworth Atheneum, Hartford

110 • Seine at Argenteuil, c. 1873
Oil on canvas, 46.5 x 65 cm
Musée d'Orsay, Paris

111 • The Road from Versailles to Louveciennes, c. 1873
Oil on canvas, 32.6 x 41.5 cm
Musée des Beaux-Arts, Lille

112 • Bust of Woman, or Before Bathing, 1873-1875
Oil on canvas, 81 x 63 cm
The Barnes Foundation, Merion

97

98

99

100

101

102

103

104

105

106

107

108

109

110

111

112

113

114

115 116

117 118

119 120

121 122 123 124

125 126 127 128

113 • The Tuileries, 1874
Oil on canvas, 225 x 300 cm
Magnin Collection, New York

114 • Seine at Argenteuil, 1874
Oil on canvas, 50 x 61 cm
The Art Museum, Portland

115 • In the Theatre Box, 1874
Oil on canvas, 27 x 22 cm
Durand-Ruel Collection, Paris

116 • The Seine at Chatou, 1874
Oil on canvas, 54 x 65 cm
Private Collection

117 • Regattas at Argenteuil, 1874
Oil on canvas, 32 x 45 cm
National Gallery of Art, Washington

118 • A Path in the Forest, 1874
Oil on canvas, 66 x 55 cm
J. C. Savior Collection, New York

**119 • Madame Monet and
Her Son, 1874**
Oil on canvas, 51 x 68 cm
National Gallery of Art, Washington

120 • The Box at the Theatre, 1874
Oil on canvas, 27 x 92 cm
Private Collection

121 • The Box at the Theatre, 1874
Oil on canvas, 80 x 64 cm
Courtauld Institute Galleries, London

122 • Dancer, 1874
Oil on canvas, 142 x 93 cm
National Gallery of Art, Washington

**123 • The Parisienne, or Lady
in Blue, 1874**
Oil on canvas, 160 x 106 cm
National Museum of Wales, Cardiff

**124 • Servant from the House
of Duval, 1874**
Oil on canvas, 101 x 71 cm
*The Metropolitan Museum of Art, New
York*

**125 • Portrait of Charles
Le Cœur, 1874**
Oil on canvas, 22 x 24 cm
Slade Collection, Beverly Hills

126 • Charles Le Cœur, 1874
Oil on canvas, 42 x 29 cm
Musée d'Orsay, Paris

127 • The Garden at Fontenay, 1874
Oil on canvas, 51 x 62 cm
*Oskar Reinhart Foundation,
Winterthur*

128 • Lady with Black Dog, 1874
Oil on canvas, 61 x 49 cm
The Tate Gallery, London

WORKS

**129 • Lady Seated
in Armchair, 1874**
Oil on canvas, 61 x 50 cm
Musée de l'Orangerie, Paris

**130 • Portrait of Madame
Henriot, 1874**
Oil on canvas, 41 x 33 cm
Simon Collection, New York

**131 • Young Woman in the
Fields, 1874**
Oil on canvas, 71 x 43 cm
Private Collection

**132 • Portrait of the
Lady, "Madame Georges
Hartmann", 1874**
Oil on canvas, 183 x 123 cm
Musée d'Orsay, Paris

133 • The Reading of Roles, 1874
Oil on canvas, 8 x 7 cm
Musée des Beaux-Arts, Reims

134 • Portrait of Alfred Sisley, 1874
Oil on canvas, 65 x 54 cm
The Art Institute, Chicago

**135 • Portrait of Nini "Gueule de
raie", 1874**
Oil on canvas, 61 x 48 cm
Private Collection

136 • Head of a Lady, 1874
Oil on canvas, 32 x 24 cm
Private Collection

**137 • The Path Through the Long
Grass, 1874**
Oil on canvas, 60 x 74 cm
Musée d'Orsay, Paris

138 • Fisherman, 1874
Oil on canvas, 54 x 65 cm
Private Collection

139 • Stormy Weather, 1874
Oil on canvas, 46 x 45 cm

**140 • On the Banks of the
River, 1874**
Oil on canvas, 54 x 65 cm
The Museum of Art, Philadelphia

141 • Seine at Argenteuil, 1874
Oil on canvas, 41 x 62 cm
Private Collection

**142 • Young Mother (The Walk),
c. 1874**
Oil on canvas, 168 x 104 cm
Frick Collection, New York

**143 • The Winter Pasture,
1874-1876**
Oil on canvas, 58.5 x 71 cm
Private Collection

144 • The Reader, c. 1874-1876
Oil on canvas, 46.5 x 38.5 cm
Musée d'Orsay, Paris

129

130

131

132

133

134

135

136

137

138

139

140

141

142

143

144

145 • Woman with Parasol and Child, c. 1874-1876
Oil on canvas, 46 x 55 cm
Museum of Fine Arts, Boston

146 • Two Apples, 1875
Oil on canvas, 13 x 25 cm
Private Collection

147 • The Banks of Seine Near Argenteuil, 1875
Oil on canvas, 53.3 x 64 cm
Private Collection

148 • English Pear Tree, 1875
Oil on canvas, 44 x 37 cm
Private Collection

149 • Child with Punch, 1875
Oil on canvas, 35 x 27 cm
Private Collection

150 • Child with Punch, 1875
Oil on canvas, 56 x 46 cm
Bostwick Collection, New York

151 • Portrait of Claude Monet, 1875
Oil on canvas, 18 x 10 cm
Musée Marmottan, Paris

152 • Portrait of Monet, 1875
Oil on canvas, 85 x 60.5 cm
Musée d'Orsay, Paris

153 • The Arbor, 1875
Oil on canvas, 81 x 65 cm
J. W. Payson Gallery of Art, Westbrook College, Portland

154 • The Spring, 1875
Oil on canvas, 130 x 78 cm
The Barnes Foundation, Merion

155 • Pierre Sisley, 1875
Oil on canvas, 26 x 21 cm
Private Collection

156 • Jeanne Sisley, 1875
Oil on canvas, 35 x 27 cm
Private Collection

157 • Woman's Portrait, 1875
Oil on canvas, 35 x 24 cm
Hahnloser Collection, Bern

158 • By the Fireplace, 1875
Oil on canvas, 61 x 50 cm
Staatsgalerie, Stuttgart

159 • The Jewish Wedding, 1875
Oil on canvas, 108 x 44 cm
Art Museum, Worcester

160 • The Pensive Woman, 1875
Oil on canvas, 46 x 38 cm
Virginia Museum of Fine Arts, Richmond

WORKS

161 • Lady Dressed for the Town, 1875
Oil on canvas, 23 x 18 cm
Marshall Field, New York

162 • Bust of a Girl, 1875
Oil on canvas, 41 x 35 cm
Private Collection

163 • Portrait of Madame Chocquet in White, 1875
Oil on canvas, 75 x 60 cm
Staatsgalerie, Stuttgart

164 • A Girl Crocheting, 1875
Oil on canvas, 74 x 59 cm
Sterling and Francine Clark Art Institute, Williamstown

165 • Blonde Girl Sewing, 1875
Oil on canvas, 46 x 35 cm
Private Collection

166 • Dress-Maker, 1875
Oil on canvas, 61 x 50 cm
Oskar Reinhart Foundation, Winterthur

167 • Self-Portrait, 1875
Oil on canvas, 38 x 31 cm
Sterling and Francine Clark Art Institute, Williamstown

168 • Portrait of Madame X, 1875
Oil on canvas, 65 x 54 cm
Bronfman Collection, Montreal

169 • Portrait of Monsieur Fournaise (Man with Pipe), 1875
Oil on canvas, 55 x 46 cm
Sterling and Francine Clark Art Institute, Williamstown

170 • The Smiling Lady (Alphonsine Fournaise), 1875
Oil on canvas, 41 x 33 cm
Museu de Arte, São Paulo

171 • Portrait of Delphine Legrand (The Attentive Girl), 1875
Oil on canvas, 81 x 60 cm
Henry P. McIlhenny Collection, Philadelphia

172 • Les Grands Boulevards, 1875
Oil on canvas, 50 x 61 cm
Henry P. McIlhenny Collection, Philadelphia

173 • The Washing Place Near Meudon, 1875
Oil on canvas, 49 x 61 cm
Sterling and Francine Clark Art Institute, Williamstown

174 • In the Park, 1875
Oil on canvas, 66 x 54 cm
Private Collection

175 • On the Banks of the River, 1875
Oil on canvas, 57.5 x 70 cm
Wildenstein Collection, New York

176 • In the Garden (Two Women Sitting on the Grass), 1875
Oil on canvas, 60 x 75 cm
The Barnes Foundation, Merion

161   162   163   164

165   166   167

168   169   170

171   172   173

174   175

176

177

178

179

180

181

182

183

184

185

186

187

188

189

190

191

192

177 • Summer, 1875
Oil on canvas, 65 x 54 cm
Musée d'Art et d'Histoire, Geneva

178 • Nini in the Garden, 1875
Oil on canvas, 61 x 50 cm
Formerly Annenberg Collection, London

179 • Girl on a Bench, 1875
Oil on canvas, 61 x 50 cm
Dr. A.C.R. Dreesmann Collection, Amsterdam

180 • Woman Sewing, 1875
Oil on canvas, 65 x 54 cm
Private Collection

181 • The Square de la Trinité, 1875
Oil on canvas, 50 x 62 cm
Private Collection

182 • Woman with a Parasol in a Garden, 1875
Oil on canvas, 54 x 65 cm
Private Collection

183 • Torso in the Sun, 1875
Oil on canvas, 81 x 65 cm
Musée d'Orsay, Paris

184 • The Bridge at Chatou, c. 1875
Oil on canvas, 50 x 65 cm
Sterling and Francine Clark Art Institute, Williamstown

185 • «Grisette», c. 1875
Oil on canvas, 41 x 32 cm
Nationalmuseum, Stockholm

186 • Girl Sitting in a Garden (La Grisette), c. 1875
Oil on canvas, 46 x 38 cm
Sterling and Francine Clark Art Institute, Williamstown

187 • Woman Knitting, c. 1875
Oil on canvas, 46 x 28 cm
Private Collection

188 • Girl with Hoop, c. 1875
Oil on canvas, 50 x 61 cm
The Museum of Art, Baltimore

189 • Girl with Dog, c. 1875
Oil on canvas, 31 x 23 cm
Private Collection

190 • Madame Henriot in Theatrical Dress, c. 1875
Oil on canvas, 161 x 104 cm
Gallery of Fine Arts, Columbus

191 • The Lovers, c. 1875
Oil on canvas, 175 x 130 cm
Národni Galeri, Prague

192 • Woman Sitting in a Garden, c. 1875
Oil on canvas, 10 x 8.5 cm
Musée d'Orsay, Paris

WORKS

193 • Woman with Veil, c. 1875
Oil on canvas, 61 x 51 cm
Musée d'Orsay, Paris

194 • Woman at the Piano, c. 1875
Oil on canvas, 93 x 74 cm
The Art Institute, Chicago

195 • Snowy Landscape, c. 1875
Oil on canvas, 51 x 66 cm
Musée de l'Orangerie, Paris

**196 • Portrait of Jacques-Eugène
Spuller, c. 1875-1876**
Oil on canvas, 46.5 x 38.5 cm
Private Collection

197 • Farm, c. 1875-1877
Oil on canvas, 46 x 56 cm
Private Collection

**198 • A Young Man (Georgres
Rivière?) and a Young Woman,
c. 1875-1880**
Oil on canvas, 31 x 45 cm
Musée de l'Orangerie, Paris

**199 • Nude Woman in the
Forest, 1876**
Oil on canvas, 32 x 22 cm
Private Collection

**200 • Woman with Japanese
Parasol, 1876**
Oil on canvas, 50 x 61 cm
Private Collection

201 • Lady in Black, 1876
Oil on canvas, 63 x 53 cm
*The Hermitage Museum, St.
Petersburg*

202 • Tama the Dog, 1876
Oil on canvas, 38.5 x 46 cm
*Sterling and Francine Clark Art
Institute, Williamstown*

203 • Tama the Dog, 1876
Oil on canvas, 37 x 31 cm
Private Collection

204 • Woman with Dog, 1876
Oil on canvas, 46 x 38 cm
Private Collection

205 • The Henriot Family, 1876
Oil on canvas, 114 x 163 cm
The Barnes Foundation, Merion

**206 • First Evening Out, also called
Le Café-concert, 1876**
Oil on canvas, 65 x 50 cm
The National Gallery, London

**207 • Portrait of a Woman
(Symphony in White), 1876**
Oil on canvas, 30 x 26 cm
Private Collection

**208 • Portrait of Marie-Sophie
Chocquet, 1876**
Oil on canvas, 36 x 45 cm
Gould Collection, Cannes

193   194   195

196   197

198   199   200

201   202

203   204   205

206   207   208

209

210

211

212

213

214

215

216

217

218

219

220

221

222

223

224

209 • Madame Henriot, 1876
Oil on canvas, 55 x 46 cm
Oskar Reinhart Foundation,
Winterthur

210 • Madame Henriot, 1876
Oil on canvas, 66 x 50 cm
National Gallery of Art, Washington

211 • Henriette Henriot (Girl with
Blue Ribbon), 1876
Oil on canvas, 41 x 32 cm
Private Collection

212 • Young Girl with Cat, 1876
Oil on canvas, 55 x 46 cm
National Gallery of Art, Washington

213 • Portrait of Nini Lopez, 1876
Oil on canvas, 27 x 22 cm
Schaefer Collection, Zurich

214 • Young Girl Dressed
in Black, 1876
Oil on canvas, 35 x 25 cm
Norton Simon Foundation, Pasadena

215 • Madame Edmond
Renoir, 1876
Oil on canvas, 37 x 28 cm
Private Collection

216 • Young Girl Braiding Her
Hair, 1876
Oil on canvas, 56 x 46 cm
National Gallery of Art, Washington

217 • Madame Chocquet
Reading, 1876
Oil on canvas, 65 x 54 cm
Ed. Cox Collection, Dallas

218 • Portrait of Victor
Chocquet, 1876
Oil on canvas, 46 x 37 cm
The Fogg Art Museum, Cambridge
(Massachusetts)

219 • Victor Chocquet, 1876
Oil on canvas, 46 x 36 cm
Oskar Reinhart Foundation,
Winterthur

220 • Child with Apple, 1876
Oil on canvas, 40 x 32 cm
Chalk Collection, Washington

221 • Child with Watering
Can, 1876
Oil on canvas, 100 x 73 cm
National Gallery of Art, Washington

222 • Jeanne Durand-Ruel, 1876
Oil on canvas, 113 x 74 cm
The Barnes Foundation, Merion

223 • Girl in White Playing with
Rope, 1876
Oil on canvas, 108 x 77 cm
The Barnes Foundation, Merion

224 • Madame Henriot, 1876
Oil on canvas, 24 x 20 cm
Private Collection

WORKS

225 • Self-Portrait, 1876
Oil on canvas, 73 x 57 cm
*The Fogg Art Museum, Cambridge
(Massachusetts)*

226 • Lady Dressed in Black, 1876
Oil on canvas, 60.4 x 40.4 cm
*Bayerische Staatsgemäldesammlungen,
Neue Pinakothek, Munich*

227 • Woman with Black Hat, 1876
Oil on cardboard and watercolor,
38 x 25 cm
Private Collection

**228 • Young Girl with Pink Feather
in her Hat, 1876**
Oil on canvas, 47 x 41 cm
Niarchos Collection, Paris

229 • Young Girls, 1876
Oil on canvas, 44 x 36 cm
Ny Carlsberg Glyptotek, Copenhagen

**230 • The Garden at the
Rue Cortot, 1876**
Oil on canvas, 151 x 97 cm
Carnegie Museum of Art, Pittsburgh

**231 • Spring or The
Conversation, 1876**
Oil on canvas, 61 x 50 cm
Private Collection

**232 • In the Garden:
Under the Trees of the
Moulin de la Galette, 1876**
Oil on canvas, 81 x 65 cm
Pushkin Museum, Moscow

233 • The Swing, 1876
Oil on canvas, 92 x 73 cm
Musée d'Orsay, Paris

**234 • Woman with Striped
Dress, 1876**
Oil on canvas, 61 x 50 cm
Private Collection

235 • Estelle with Red Hat, 1876
Oil on canvas, 58 x 30 cm
Private Collection

236 • Young Woman, 1876
Oil on canvas, 27 x 22 cm
*Formerly Erick Maria Remarque
Collection*

237 • The Dance, 1876
Oil on canvas, 46 x 28 cm
Private Collection

**238 • Study for Dance at the Moulin
de la Galette, 1876**
Oil on canvas, 64 x 85 cm
Ordrupgaardsamlingen, Copenhagen

239 • The Moulin de la Galette, 1876
Oil on canvas, 78 x 113 cm
Ryoei Saito Collection, Japan

**240 • Dance at the Moulin de la
Galette, 1876**
Oil on canvas, 131 x 175 cm
Musée d'Orsay, Paris

225 226 227

228 229 230

231 232 233

234 235

236 237 238

239 240

241

242

243

244

245

246

247

248

249

250

251

252

253

254

255

256

241 • Nude, 1876
Oil on canvas, 92 x 73 cm
Pushkin Museum, Moscow

242 • Bather after Swimming, 1876
Oil on canvas, 93 x 73 cm
Neue Galerie, Vienna

243 • Woman Dressing, 1876
Oil on canvas, 23 x 16 cm
Private Collection

244 • Woman with Rose, 1876
Oil on canvas, 33 x 27 cm
Private Collection

245 • Young Girl in Blue, 1876
Oil on canvas, 42 x 32 cm
Wildenstein Collection, New York

246 • Portrait of Madame Alphonse Daudet, 1876
Oil on canvas, 46 x 38 cm
Musée d'Orsay, Paris

247 • The Seine at Champrosay, 1876
Oil on canvas, 55 x 66 cm
Musée d'Orsay, Paris

248 • Mademoiselle Georgette Charpentier, Seated, 1876
Oil on canvas, 98 x 73 cm
Private Collection

249 • Man on Stairs, 1876
Oil on canvas, 165 x 63 cm
Formerly Gerstenberg Collection, Berlin

250 • The Cup of Chocolate, 1876
Oil on canvas, 165 x 63 cm
Formerly Gerstenberg Collection, Berlin

251 • Profile of a Blonde (Portrait of Nini Lopez), 1876
Oil on canvas, 26 x 22 cm
Private Collection

252 • Portrait of Nini Lopez, 1876
Oil on canvas, 54 x 38 cm
Private Collection

253 • Naiad, 1876
Oil on canvas, 27 x 22 cm
Private Collection

254 • Bather, 1876
Oil on canvas, 35 x 27 cm
Bukpot Collection, Brussels

255 • The Artist's Studio, Rue Saint-Georges, 1876
Oil on canvas, 46 x 38 cm
Norton Simon Foundation, Pasadena

256 • Portrait of Young Woman, 1876
Oil on canvas, 27 x 22 cm
Private Collection

WORKS

257 • Flowers Reflected in Mirror, 1876
Oil on canvas, 93 • x 72 cm
Rothschild Collection, Paris

258 • Young Girl with Cat, 1876
Oil on canvas, 33 x 25 cm
Private Collection

259 • Mademoiselle Henriot, 1876
Oil on canvas, 30 x 26 cm
Formerly Santamarina Collection, Buenos Aires

260 • Path Through the Long Grass, 1876
Oil on canvas, 54 x 65 cm
Private Collection

261 • Leaving the Conservatory, 1876-1877
Oil on canvas, 187 x 117 cm
The Barnes Foundation, Merion

262 • Portrait of Madame Georges Charpentier, c. 1876-1877
Oil on canvas, 46.5 x 38 cm
Musée d'Orsay, Paris

263 • Young Woman Seated (La Pensée), c. 1876-1877
Oil on canvas, 66 x 55 cm
British Government, London

264 • Pivoines, 1876-1878
Oil on canvas, 59 x 50 cm
Private Collection

265 • Portrait called Portrait of Margot, c. 1876-1878
Oil on canvas, 46.5 x 38 cm
Musée d'Orsay, Paris

266 • Spring Landscape, 1877
Oil on canvas, 38 x 53 cm
National Museum of Fine Arts, Algiers

267 • At the Café, 1877
Oil on canvas, 39 x 35 cm
Scharf Collection, Hamburg

268 • Jeanne Samary, 1877
Oil on canvas, 46 x 40 cm
Comédie-Française, Paris

269 • Portrait of the Actress Jeanne Samary, 1877
Oil on canvas, 56 x 46 cm
Pushkin Museum, Moscow

270 • Head of a Woman, 1877
Oil on cement, 30 cm
O'Hana Gallery, London

271 • Head of a Woman, 1877
Oil on cement, 132 x 60 cm
Private Collection

272 • Portrait of Margot, 1877
Oil on canvas, 32 x 25 cm
Private Collection

273 • Woman Reading, 1877
Oil on canvas, 63 x 53 cm
Weysson Seyburn Collection, Detroit

257　258　259
260　261　262
263　264　265
266　267　268
269　270　271

272　273

274

275

276

277

278

279

280

281

282

283

284

285

286

287

288

274 • Couple Reading, 1877
Oil on canvas, 32 x 24 cm
Private Collection

**275 • Monsieur and Madame
Benjamin Godard, 1877**
Oil on canvas, 35 x 27 cm
Reves Collection, Roquebrune

**276 • The Countess of
Pourtalès, 1877**
Oil on canvas, 94 x 73 cm
Museu de Arte, São Paulo

**277 • Portrait of Eugène
Murer, 1877**
Oil on canvas, 46 x 39 cm
Haupt Collection, New York

278 • Portrait of Paul Murer, 1877
Oil on canvas, 46 x 36 cm
Private Collection

279 • Portrait of Marie Murer, 1877
Oil on canvas, 68 x 57 cm
National Gallery of Art, Washington

280 • Portrait of Marie Murer, 1877
Oil on canvas, 65 x 50 cm
The Barnes Foundation, Merion

281 • Young Soldier, 1877
Oil on canvas, 54 x 32 cm
National Gallery of Art, Washington

282 • Reflection, 1877
Oil on canvas, 46 x 38 cm
Private Collection

283 • Woman Reading, 1877
Oil on canvas, 41 x 32 cm
Whitney Collection, New York

**284 • Portrait of a Romanian
Woman (Madame Iscovesco), 1877**
Oil on canvas, 41 x 33 cm
Ordrupgaardsamlingen, Copenhagen

**285 • Portrait of Georges
Rivière, 1877**
Oil on cement, 36 x 29 cm
National Gallery of Art, Washington

286 • Woman with Lilac, 1877
Oil on canvas, 73 x 60 cm
Payson Collection, New York

287 • Girl in a Boat, 1877
Oil on canvas, 73 x 92 cm
Private Collection

288 • Head of a Young Girl, 1877
Oil on canvas, 32 x 26 cm
Wildenstein Collection, Tokyo

WORKS

289 • Paysage, 1877
Oil on canvas, 39 x 46 cm

290 • Young Girl (L'Ingénue), c. 1877
Oil on canvas, 55 x 46 cm
Sterling and Francine Clark Art Institute, Williamstown

291 • Head of a Woman, c. 1877
Oil on cement, 26 cm
Private Collection

292 • Woman Crocheting, c. 1877
Oil on canvas, 40 x 32 cm
The Barnes Foundation, Merion

293 • Portrait of the Baron Barbier, c. 1877
Oil on canvas, 16 x 15 cm
Private Collection

294 • Man with Small Hat, c. 1877
Oil on canvas, 29 x 28 cm
Private Collection

295 • At the Café (Michel de l'Hay), c. 1877
Oil on canvas, 40 x 17 cm
Private Collection

296 • The Café, c. 1877
Oil on canvas, 34 x 26 cm
Rijksmuseum Kröller-Müller, Otterlo

297 • Young Girl with Bunch of Tulips, 1878
Oil on canvas, 55 x 46 cm
Private Collection

298 • The Café, 1878
Oil on canvas, 100 x 81 cm
Private Collection

299 • At the Milliner's, 1878
Oil on canvas, 33 x 23 cm
The Fogg Art Museum, Cambridge (Massachusetts)

300 • Confidences (The Inseparable Women), 1878
Oil on canvas, 61 x 50 cm
Oskar Reinhart Foundation, Winterthur

301 • Jeanne Samary, 1878
Oil on canvas, 173 x 102 cm
The Hermitage Museum, St. Petersburg

302 • Madame Charpentier and Her Children, 1878
Oil on canvas, 153 x 190 cm
The Metropolitan Museum of Art, New York

303 • Portrait of Monsieur Lestringuez, 1878
Oil on canvas, 40 x 31 cm
Private Collection

304 • Portrait of Monsieur Lestringuez, 1878
Oil on canvas, 55 x 64 cm
Private Collection

289   290   291

292   293   294

295   296   297   298

299   300   301

302

303   304

305

306

307

308

309

310

311

312

313

314

315

316

317

318

319

320

305 • Portrait of an Old Woman, 1878
Oil on canvas, 44 x 37 cm
Private Collection

306 • Landscape in Pourville, 1878
Oil on canvas, 46 x 54 cm
The Barnes Foundation, Merion

307 • Portrait of Jeanne Samary, 1878
Oil on canvas, 41 x 32 cm
Private Collection

308 • Roses and Honeysuckle, 1878
Oil on canvas, 81 x 65 cm
Private Collection

309 • Bouquet in Vase, 1878
Oil on canvas, 47 x 32 cm
Museum of Art, Indianapolis

310 • Spring at Chatou, c. 1878
Oil on canvas, 60 x 74 cm
Formerly Lady Aberconway Collection, London

311 • Parasol, c. 1878
Oil on canvas, 61 x 50 cm
Treat Paine Collection, Boston

312 • Portrait of Young Girl, c. 1878
Oil on canvas, 46 x 38 cm
Private Collection

313 • Bouquet of Lilacs, c. 1878
Oil on canvas, 65 x 54 cm
Niarchos Collection, Paris

314 • Cutting Flowers, c. 1878-1890
Oil on canvas, 51 x 63 cm
The Art Institute, Chicago

315 • Bust of Nude Woman, 1879
Oil on canvas, 56 x 38 cm
Private Collection

316 • Two Little Circus Girls, 1879
Oil on canvas, 135 x 99.5 cm
The Art Institute, Chicago

317 • The Conversation, 1879
Oil on canvas, 45 x 38 cm
Nationalmuseum, Stockholm

318 • Conversation, 1879
Oil on canvas, 45 x 38 cm
Private Collection

319 • Portrait of the Artist, 1879
Oil on canvas, 19 x 14 cm
Musée d'Orsay, Paris

320 • Lady Sewing, 1879
Oil on canvas, 61 x 50 cm
The Art Institute, Chicago

WORKS

321 • Woman's Portrait, 1879
Oil on canvas, 42 x 31 cm
Private Collection

322 • Little Margot Bérard, 1879
Oil on canvas, 41 x 33 cm
The Metropolitan Museum of Art, New York

323 • Little André Bérard , 1879
Oil on canvas, 40 x 32 cm
Private Collection

324 • Portrait of Thérèse Bérard, 1879
Oil on canvas, 55 x 46 cm
Sterling and Francine Clark Art Institute, Williamstown

325 • Portrait of Madame Paul Bérard, 1879
Oil on canvas, 80 x 79 cm
Musée de Dieppe, Dieppe

326 • Marthe Bérard, the Girl with the Blue Belt, 1879
Oil on canvas, 130 x 75 cm
Museu de Arte, São Paulo

327 • The Little Fisher Girl, 1879
Oil on canvas, 60 x 45 cm
Private Collection

328 • The Little Fisher Girl, 1879
Oil on canvas, 61 x 46 cm
Private Collection

329 • Schoolboy, 1879
Oil on canvas, 61 x 46 cm
Private Collection

330 • Scene from Tannhäuser (Act I), 1879
Oil on canvas, 37 x 142 cm
Private Collection

331 • Study from Tannhäuser, 1879
Oil on canvas, 55 x 66 cm
Sterling and Francine Clark Art Institute, Williamstown

332 • Scene from Tannhäuser (Act III), 1879
Oil on canvas, 57 x 142 cm
Private Collection

333 • Scene from Tannhaüser (Act I), 1879
Oil on canvas, 50 x 135 cm
Salabert Collection, Paris

334 • Scene from Tannhaüser (Act III), 1879
Oil on canvas, 50 x 135 cm
Salabert Collection, Paris

335 • La Petite Bohémienne (Gypsy Girl), 1879
Oil on canvas, 73 x 54 cm
Private Collection

336 • The Cliffs Near Dieppe, 1879
Oil on canvas, 50 x 60 cm
Private Collection

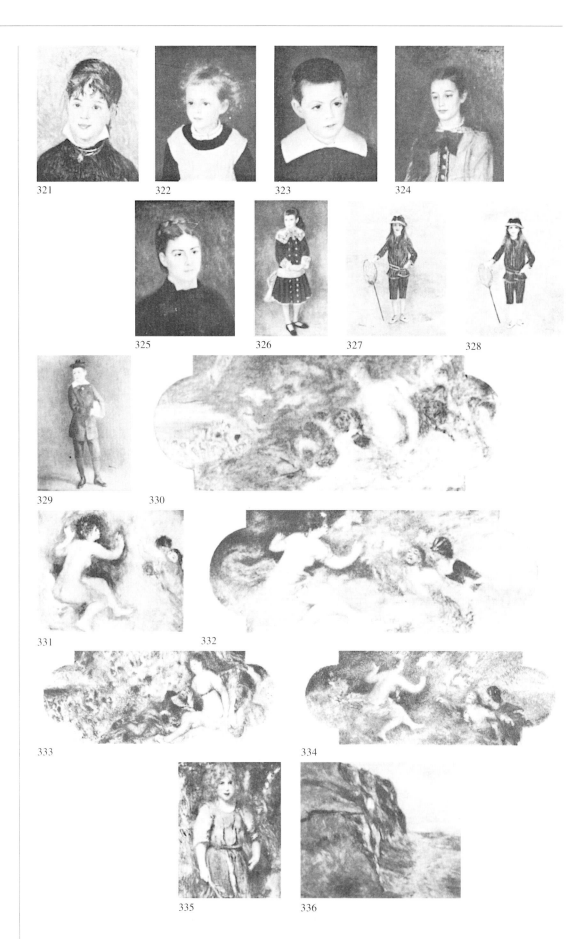

321 322 323 324

325 326 327 328

329 330

331 332

333 334

335 336

337

338

339

340

341

342

343

344

345

346

347

348

349

350

351

352

WORKS

353 • The Bouquet, 1879
Oil on canvas, 82.5 x 64.5 cm
*Sterling and Francine Clark Art
Institute, Williamstown*

354 • Roses in Glass Vase, 1879
Oil on canvas, 66 x 55 cm
Peralta-Ramos Collection

**355 • On the Banks of the
River, 1879**
Oil on canvas, 55 x 66 cm
Private Collection

356 • The Sea at Berneval, 1879
Oil on canvas, 54 x 65 cm

357 • Wheat Field, 1879
Oil on canvas, 50 x 61 cm

358 • The Road, 1879
Oil on canvas, 54 x 66 cm

359 • Man's Portrait, c. 1879
Oil on canvas, 32 x 23 cm
The Barnes Foundation, Merion

360 • Man's Portrait, c. 1879
Oil on canvas, 20 x 19 cm
Private Collection

**361 • The Villa of Blanche Pierson
at Pourville, c. 1879**
Oil on canvas, 54 x 65 cm
Private Collection

**362 • Seine at Asnières (La Yole),
c. 1879**
Oil on canvas, 71 x 92 cm
The National Gallery, London

**363 • The Oarsman of Bougival,
c. 1879**
Oil on canvas, 41 x 33 cm
Lévy-Ditisheim, Basel

**364 • Portrait of Edmond Renoir,
c. 1879**
Oil on canvas, 32 x 23 cm
Private Collection

**365 • Nude Woman Standing,
c. 1879**
Oil on canvas, 34 x 21 cm
Private Collection

366 • Near the Lake, c. 1879-1880
Oil on canvas, 46.2 x 55.4 cm
The Art Institute, Chicago

**367 • The Oarsmen (Breakfast on
the Banks of the River), c. 1879**
Oil on canvas, 54.7 x 65.5 cm
The Art Institute, Chicago

368 • Seine at Bougival, c. 1879
Oil on canvas, 32 x 41 cm
Private Collection

353

354

355

356

357

358

359

360

361

362

363

364

365

366

367

368

369

370

371

372

373

374

375

376

377

378

379

380

381

382

383

384

369 • In the Forest, 1880
Oil on canvas, 56 x 46 cm
Museum of Western Art, Tokyo

**370 • At the Concert
(In the Box), 1880**
Oil on canvas, 99 x 80 cm
*Sterling and Francine Clark Art
Institute, Williamstown*

**371 • Sketch of the Place
Clichy, 1880**
Oil on canvas, 36 x 28 cm
Private Collection

**372 • Sketch of the Place
Clichy, 1880**
Oil on canvas, 55.5 x 38.5 cm
Bührle Collection, Zurich

373 • The Place Clichy, 1880
Oil on canvas, 32 x 24 cm
Hornby Collection, London

**374 • Madame Renoir with
a Dog, 1880**
Oil on canvas, 32 x 41 cm
Private Collection

375 • Young Girl Sleeping, 1880
Oil on canvas, 120 x 94 cm
*Sterling and Francine Clark Art
Institute, Williamstown*

376 • Girl with Fan, 1880
Oil on canvas, 65 x 50 cm
*The Hermitage Museum,
St. Petersburg*

377 • Girl Smiling, 1880
Oil on canvas, 28 x 21 cm
Private Collection

378 • Nude, 1880
Oil on canvas, 80 x 65 cm
Musée Rodin, Paris

**379 • Madame Adela O Campo de
Heimendahl, 1880**
Oil on canvas, 66 x 55 cm
*O Campo de Casares-Lumb
Collection, Buenos Aires*

380 • Georges Rivière, 1880
Oil on canvas, 40 x 38 cm
Private Collection

381 • The First Step, 1880
Oil on canvas, 111 x 81 cm
Private Collection

**382 • Madame Fould (Woman with
Ruff), 1880**
Oil on canvas, 55 x 46 cm
Private Collection

383 • Woman with White Ruff, 1880
Oil on canvas, 46.3 x 38 cm
Musée d'Orsay, Paris

**384 • Portrait of the Young
Bergeret, 1880**
Oil on canvas, 40 x 32 cm
Museum of Fine Arts, Boston

WORKS

385 • Fernand Halphen, 1880
Oil on canvas, 46 x 38 cm
Halphen Collection

386 • Paul Bérard, 1880
Oil on canvas, 81 x 65 cm
Private Collection

387 • View of the Coast Near Wargemont, 1880
Oil on canvas, 50 x 62 cm
The Metropolitan Museum of Art, New York

388 • The Road to Berneval, 1880
Oil on canvas, 50 x 60 cm

389 • Mademoiselle Fournaise, 1880
Oil on canvas, 46 x 38 cm
Private Collection

390 • Mademoiselle Grimprel in Blue Lace, 1880
Oil on canvas, 45 x 35 cm
Javal Collection, Paris

391 • Mademoiselle Grimprel in Red Lace, 1880
Oil on canvas, 45 x 35 cm
Javal Collection, Paris

392 • Maurice Grimprel, 1880
Oil on canvas, 54.9 x 38.1 cm
Straus Collection, New York

393 • Mademoiselle Irène Cahen d'Anvers, 1880
Oil on canvas, 65 x 54 cm
Bührle Collection, Zurich

394 • Girl with a Falcon (Mlle Fleury in Algerian Costume), 1880
Oil on canvas, 126 x 78 cm
Sterling and Francine Clark Art Institute, Williamstown

395 • Girl with Hat Adorned with Wildflowers, 1880
Oil on canvas, 55 x 46 cm
Ortiz-Linarès Collection, Paris

396 • Young Girl Reading, 1880
Oil on canvas, 55 x 46 cm
Städelsches Kunstinstitut und Städtische Galerie, Frankfurt

397 • Portrait of a Young Woman, 1880
Oil on canvas, 17 x 14 cm
Private Collection

398 • Bust of a Woman, 1880
Oil on canvas, 36 x 34 cm
The Hermitage Museum, St. Petersburg

399 • Young Girl Seated, 1880
Oil on canvas, 62 x 50 cm
Cushing Collection, New York

400 • Young Girl Sleeping, 1880
Oil on canvas, 49 x 60 cm
Private Collection

385

386

387

388

389

390

391

392

393

394

395

396

397

398

399

400

401

402

403

404

405

406

407

408

409

410

411

412

413

414

415

416

401 • Two Figures on the Cliff, 1880
Oil on canvas, 26 x 46 cm

402 • The Meadow, 1880
Oil on canvas, 46 x 26 cm

403 • Géraniums in a Copper Vessel, 1880
Oil on canvas, 81 x 64 cm
Private Collection

404 • Peonies, 1880
Oil on canvas, 65 x 54 cm
Sterling and Francine Clark Art Institute, Williamstown

405 • Bather Seated on a Rock, 1880
Oil on canvas, 50 x 40 cm
Hausamann Collection, Zurich

406 • Woman with Straw Hat, 1880
Oil on canvas, 50 x 61 cm
Private Collection

407 • Fish, 1880
Oil on canvas, 41.5 x 54 cm
Kunsthaus, Zurich

408 • Three Partridges, 1880
Oil on canvas, 31 x 40 cm

409 • Place Clichy, c. 1880
Oil on canvas, 64 x 54 cm
Fitzwilliam Museum, Cambridge

410 • The Laundress, c. 1880
Oil on canvas, 81 x 56 cm
The Art Institute, Chicago

411 • Monsieur Bernard with Felt Hat, Profile, c. 1880
Oil on canvas, 40 x 32 cm
Bayerische Staatsgemäldesammlungen, Neue Pinakothek, Munich

412 • Monsieur Bernard with Felt Hat, Front View, c. 1880
Oil on canvas, 40 x 32 cm
Private Collection

413 • Roses and Dahlias, c. 1880
Oil on canvas, 39 x 61 cm
Thannhauser Foundation, New York

414 • Vase of Roses, c. 1880
Oil on canvas, 65 x 53 cm
Private Collection

415 • Woman Reading an Illustrated Magazine, 1880-1881
Oil on canvas, 47 x 56 cm
Museum of Art, Rhode Island School of Design, Providence

416 • Young Woman in Blue, 1880-1881
Oil on canvas, 41 x 32 cm
Eisner Collection, New York

417 • The Luncheon of the Boating Party, 1880-1881
Oil on canvas, 130 x 173 cm
The Phillips Collection, Washington

418 • The Vase of Chrysanthemums, 1880-1882
Oil on canvas, 82 x 65.5 cm
Private Collection

419 • Chrysanthemums, 1880-1882
Oil on canvas, 55 x 54 cm
Formerly Annenberg Collection, London

420 • Onions, 1881
Oil on canvas, 40 x 60 cm
Sterling and Francine Clark Art Institute, Williamstown

421 • Girl with a Fan, 1881
Oil on canvas, 65 x 54 cm
Sterling and Francine Clark Art Institute, Williamstown

422 • Bust of Woman with Hat, 1881
Oil on canvas, 32 x 24 cm
Private Collection

423 • The Cahen d'Anvers Girls, 1881
Oil on canvas, 119 x 74 cm
Museu de Arte, São Paulo

424 • Bust of a Child, 1881
Oil on canvas, 37 x 32 cm
Private Collection

425 • Algerian Woman Seated, 1881
Oil on canvas, 51 x 41 cm
Museum of Fine Arts, Boston

426 • Banana Plantation, 1881
Oil on canvas, 51.5 x 63.5 cm
Musée d'Orsay, Paris

427 • The Mosque (Arab Celebration), 1881
Oil on canvas, 73 x 92 cm
Musée d'Orsay, Paris

428 • The Bay of Algiers, 1881
Oil on canvas, 51 x 65 cm
Private Collection

429 • Arab Mounted on a Camel, 1881
Oil on canvas, 73 x 76 cm
Paley Collection, New York

430 • Young Algerian Girl Leaning, 1881
Oil on canvas, 41 x 32 cm
Private Collection

431 • Madame Renoir, 1881
Oil on canvas, 24 x 20 cm
Private Collection

432 • Portrait of Douglas Fitch, 1881
Oil on canvas, 24 x 19 cm
Private Collection

417

418

419

420

421

422

423

424

425

426

427

428

429

430

431

432

433

434

435

436

437

438

439

440

441

442

443

444

445

446

447

448

433 • The Railway Bridge at Chatou, or The Pink Chestnut Trees, 1881
Oil on canvas, 54 x 65.5 cm
Musée d'Orsay, Paris

434 • On the Terrace, 1881
Oil on canvas, 100 x 80 cm
The Art Institute, Chicago

435 • Still Life with Peaches and Grapes, 1881
Oil on canvas, 52 x 63 cm
The Metropolitan Museum of Art, New York

436 • Still Life with Peaches, 1881
Oil on canvas, 53.3 x 64.7 cm
The Metropolitan Museum of Art, New York

437 • Chestnut Trees in Flower, 1881
Oil on canvas, 71 x 89 cm
Nationalgalerie, Staatliche Museen, Berlin

438 • Girl with Blue Hat, 1881
Oil on canvas, 40 x 35 cm
Private Collection

439 • Sketches of Heads (The Berard children), 1881
Oil on canvas, 62 x 83 cm
Sterling and Francine Clark Art Institute, Williamstown

440 • Alfred Bérard and His Dog, 1881
Oil on canvas, 65 x 51 cm
The Museum of Art, Philadelphia

441 • Albert Cahen d'Anvers, 1881
Oil on canvas, 81 x 65 cm
Private Collection

442 • Venice: Gondola on the Grand Canal, 1881
Oil on canvas, 65 x 54 cm
Kramarsky Collection, New York

443 • Venice, Fog, 1881
Oil on canvas, 45 x 63 cm
Kreeger Collection, Washington

444 • On the Grand Canal, Venice, 1881
Oil on canvas, 54 x 65 cm
Museum of Fine Arts, Boston

445 • Venice: The Doges' Palace in Venice, 1881
Oil on canvas, 54.5 x 65 cm
Sterling and Francine Clark Art Institute, Williamstown

446 • St. Mark's, Venice, 1881
Oil on canvas, 65.4 x 81.3 cm
The Institute of Arts, Minneapolis

447 • Venetian Woman, 1881
Oil on canvas, 35 x 27 cm
Private Collection

448 • Southern Fruit, 1881
Oil on canvas, 51 x 68.5 cm
The Art Institute, Chicago

WORKS

449 • Capo di Monte and Sorrente, Bay of Naples, 1881
Oil on canvas, 53 x 65 cm
Durand-Ruel Collection, Paris

450 • Landscape of Calabria, 1881
Oil on canvas, 42 x 52 cm
Durand-Ruel Collection, Paris

451 • Vesuvius, 1881
Oil on canvas, 57 x 80 cm
Sterling and Francine Clark Art Institute, Williamstown

452 • The Bay of Naples, 1881
Oil on canvas, 59.7 x 81.3 cm
The Metropolitan Museum of Art, New York

453 • View of Naples, 1881
Oil on canvas, 48 x 64 cm
Private Collection

454 • Head of a Young Neopolitan Girl, 1881
Oil on canvas, 36 x 31 cm
The Museum of Fine Arts, Montreal

455 • Young Mother (The Child's Toilet), 1881
Oil on canvas, 120 x 84 cm
The Barnes Foundation, Merion

456 • Italian with Tambourine, 1881
Oil on canvas, 77 x 32 cm
Rosengart Collection, Lucerne

457 • Head of Woman, 1881
Oil on canvas, 11 x 9 cm
Private Collection

458 • Head of Young Italian Woman, 1881
Oil on canvas, 46 x 37 cm
Private Collection

459 • Blonde Bather, Fog, 1881
Oil on canvas, 82 x 66 cm
Sterling and Francine Clark Art Institute, Williamstown

460 • Woman Dancing in Italian Costume, 1881
Oil on canvas, 41 x 32 cm
Private Collection

461 • Algerian Woman, 1881
Oil on canvas, 41.3 x 32.2 cm
Private Collection

462 • Algerian Landscape, the Ravine of La Femme Sauvage, 1881
Oil on canvas, 65.5 x 81 cm
Musée d'Orsay, Paris

463 • Garden in Algiers, 1881
Oil on canvas, 81 x 65 cm
Private Collection

464 • Venice: Gondola on the Grand Canal, 1881
Oil on canvas, 59.5 x 75 cm
Private Collection

449   450

451   452

453   454   455   456

457   458   459

460   461   462

463   464

465

466

467

468

469

470

471

472

473

474

475

476

477

478

479

480

465 • The Seine at Chatou, c. 1881
Oil on canvas, 74 x 92 cm
Museum of Fine Arts, Boston

466 • Rowing at Bougival, c. 1881
Oil on canvas, 54 x 65 cm
The Barnes Foundation, Merion

467 • Girls in Black, c. 1881
Oil on canvas, 80 x 65 cm
Pushkin Museum, Moscow

468 • Woman with Hat, c. 1881
Oil on canvas, 47 x 36 cm
Private Collection

469 • Peaches, c. 1881-1882
Oil on canvas, 38 x 47 cm
Musée de l'Orangerie, Paris

470 • The Umbrellas, 1881-1885
Oil on canvas, 180 x 115 cm
The National Gallery, London

471 • Richard Wagner, 1882
Oil on canvas, 53 x 46 cm
Musée d'Orsay, Paris

**472 • Bust of a Nude Young
Girl , 1882**
Oil on canvas, 38 x 29 cm
Private Collection

473 • The Rocks at L'Estaque, 1882
Oil on canvas, 31 x 40 cm
Private Collection

**474 • Rocky Crags at
L'Estaque, 1882**
Oil on canvas, 66 x 82 cm
Museum of Fine Arts, Boston

475 • Olive Trees at L'Estaque, 1882
Oil on canvas, 37 x 67 cm
Private Collection

476 • Mosque in Algiers, 1882
Oil on canvas, 49 x 60 cm
Private Collection

**477 • Algerian Woman with Her
Child, 1882**
Oil on canvas, 41 x 32 cm
Private Collection

478 • Algerian Woman Seated, 1882
Oil on canvas, 55 x 46 cm
Private Collection

479 • Algerian Figures, 1882
Oil on canvas, 25 x 40 cm
National Museum of Fine Arts, Algiers

480 • Ali. Arab Child, 1882
Oil on canvas, 52 x 28 cm
Brody Collection, Los Angeles

WORKS

481 • Algerian Boy, 1882
Oil on canvas, 17 x 15 cm
Muss Collection, New York

482 • Old Arab Woman, 1882
Oil on canvas, 30 x 24 cm
Tweed Collection, New York

483 • Old Arab Woman, 1882
Oil on canvas, 24 x 16 cm
Private Collection

**484 • Study of Algerian
Figures, 1882**
Oil on canvas, 69 x 60 cm

485 • Torso of a Nude Woman, 1882
Oil on canvas, 16 x 11 cm
Private Collection

486 • Joseph Durand-Ruel, 1882
Oil on canvas, 81 x 65 cm
Durand-Ruel Collection, Paris

**487 • Mademoiselle Marie-Thérèse
Durand-Ruel Sewing, 1882**
Oil on canvas, 65 x 54 cm
*Sterling and Francine Clark Art
Institute, Williamstown*

**488 • Portrait of Charles and
Georges Durand-Ruel, 1882**
Oil on canvas, 65 x 81 cm
Durand-Ruel Collection, Paris

**489 • The Daughters of Paul
Durand-Ruel, 1882**
Oil on canvas, 81 x 65 cm
The Chrysler Museum, Norfolk

490 • Madame Hériot, 1882
Oil on canvas, 65 x 54 cm
Kunsthalle, Hamburg

**491 • Bust of Woman and
Still Life, 1882**
Oil on canvas, 22 x 16 cm
Private Collection

492 • Mademoiselle Demarsy, 1882
Oil on canvas, 61 x 51 cm
Harriman Collection, New York

**493 • Among the Roses (Madame
Léon Clapisson), 1882**
Oil on canvas, 100 x 81 cm
Clark Collection, New York

494 • Green Garden, 1882
Oil on canvas, 92 x 68 cm
Museum of Art, Toledo (Ohio)

495 • Lady with Cat, 1882
Oil on canvas, 100 x 81 cm
Wrightsman Collection, New York

496 • Head of a Young Girl, 1882
Oil on canvas, 22 x 17 cm
Garlish Collection, New York

481

482

483

484

485

486

487

488

489

490

491

492

493

494

495

496

497 498 499

500 501 502

503 504

505 506

507 508 509

510 511 512 513

497 • Woman with White Tulle Bow, 1882
Oil on canvas, 55 x 46 cm
Mahmoud Khalil Bey Museum, Cairo

498 • Bather Seated, 1882
Oil on canvas, 54 x 39 cm
Private Collection

499 • Head of a Child, 1882
Oil on canvas, 25 x 22 cm
Kunstmuseum, St Gall

500 • Souvenir of Algiers, 1882
Oil on canvas, 32 x 41 cm
Durand-Ruel Collection, Paris

501 • Landscape with Bathing Boys, 1882
Oil on canvas, 53 x 64 cm
Private Collection

502 • Bather Seated on a Rock, 1882
Oil on canvas, 54 x 39 cm
Musée Marmottan, Paris

503 • Seated on the Woodpile, 1882
Oil on canvas, 65 x 54 cm
Friedland Collection, New York

504 • Madame Clapisson, 1882
Oil on canvas, 21 x 18 cm
Danforth Collection, Providence

505 • Head of a Young Girl, 1882
Oil on canvas, 32 x 25 cm
Private Collection

506 • The Sea, 1882
Oil on canvas, 54 x 65 cm

507 • The Melon, 1882
Oil on canvas, 54.5 x 65 cm
Private Collection

508 • Chrysanthemums, c. 1882
Oil on canvas, 54.7 x 66.1 cm
The Art Institute, Chicago

509 • Steps at Algiers, c. 1882
Oil on canvas, 73 x 60.5 cm
Private Collection

510 • Bather (Blonde Bather II), c. 1882
Oil on canvas, 90 x 63 cm
Private Collection

511 • Dance at Bougival, 1882-1883
Oil on canvas, 182 x 98 cm
Museum of Fine Arts, Boston

512 • Dance in the City, 1882-1883
Oil on canvas, 180 x 90 cm
Musée d'Orsay, Paris

513 • Dance in the Country, 1882-1883
Oil on canvas, 180 x 90 cm
Musée d'Orsay, Paris

WORKS

514 • The Plate of Plums, 1882-1884
Oil on canvas, 56 x 46 cm
Private Collection

515 • Portrait of Charlotte Berthier, called Madame Caillebotte, 1883
Oil on canvas, 92 x 73 cm
National Gallery of Art, Washington

516 • Portrait of Léon Clapisson, 1883
Oil on canvas, 32 x 15 cm
Private Collection

517 • Portrait of Madame Clapisson, 1883
Oil on canvas, 82 x 65 cm
The Art Institute, Chicago

518 • Young Girl in Blue, 1883
Oil on canvas, 54 x 35 cm
National Museum of Wales, Cardiff

519 • The Algerian, 1883
Oil on canvas, 37 x 32 cm
Private Collection

520 • Young Girl with Parasol (Aline Nunès), 1883
Oil on canvas, 130.2 x 80 cm
Private Collection

521 • Young Boy on the Beach at Yport (Robert Nunès), 1883
Oil on canvas, 130.2 x 80 cm
The Barnes Foundation, Merion

522 • Child in White Dress (Lucie Bérard), 1883
Oil on canvas, 61 x 50 cm
The Art Institute, Chicago

523 • Low Tide at Yport, 1883
Oil on canvas, 54 x 65 cm

524 • The Haycocks, 1883
Oil on canvas, 21.5 x 32 cm

525 • Grass on the Banks of the Seine, 1883
Oil on canvas, 53 x 65 cm
Roëll-Kissler Collection, Bilthoven

526 • Melon and Apples, 1883
Oil on canvas, 37 x 54 cm
Oskar Reinhart Foundation, Winterthur

527 • Apples in a Fruit Basket, 1883
Oil on canvas, 54 x 65 cm
Sterling and Francine Clark Art Institute, Williamstown

528 • Nude on the Beach, 1883
Oil on canvas, 65 x 81 cm
Haupt Collection, New York

529 • Sunset by the Sea , 1883
Oil on canvas, 53 x 66 cm
Sterling and Francine Clark Art Institute, Williamstown

514

515

516

517

518

519

520

521

522

523

524

525

526

527

528

529

530

531

532

533

534

535

536

537

538

539

540

541

542

543

544

530 • Landscape at Guernsey, 1883
Oil on canvas, 46 x 56 cm
Sterling and Francine Clark Art Institute, Williamstown

531 • Guernsey, 1883
Oil on canvas, 19 x 33 cm

532 • The Sea at Guernsey, 1883
Oil on canvas, 54 x 65 cm
Sterling and Francine Clark Art Institute, Williamstown

533 • Moulin Huet Bay in Guernsey, 1883
Oil on canvas, 46.1 x 65.4 cm
The Metropolitan Museum of Art, New York

534 • Moulin Huet Bay in Guernsey, 1883
Oil on canvas, 46 x 55 cm
Private Collection

535 • Mist on Guernsey, 1883
Oil on canvas, 54 x 65 cm
Private Collection

536 • By the Seashore, 1883
Oil on canvas, 92 x 73 cm
The Metropolitan Museum of Art, New York

537 • Beach on Guernsey, 1883
Oil on canvas, 46 x 55 cm
Private Collection

538 • Children by Sea in Guernsey, 1883
Oil on canvas, 91.5 x 66.5 cm
Museum of Fine Arts, Boston

539 • Children by sea in Guernsey, 1883
Oil on canvas, 54 x 65 cm
The Barnes Foundation, Merion

540 • The Sea, Guernsey, 1883
Oil on canvas, 46 x 56 cm
Musée d'Orsay, Paris

541 • Beach in Guernsey, 1883
Oil on canvas, 46 x 55 cm
Private Collection

542 • Bathers in Guernsey, 1883
Oil on canvas, 46 x 38 cm
Private Collection

543 • Bathers in Guernsey, 1883
Oil on canvas, 38 x 46 cm
Private Collection

544 • Nude in a Landscape, 1883
Oil on canvas, 65 x 52 cm
Musée de l'Orangerie, Paris

WORKS

545 • Landscape Near Menton, 1883
Oil on canvas, 66 x 81.5 cm
Museum of Fine Arts, Boston

546 • Girl with Chignon, 1883
Oil on canvas, 54 x 44.5 cm
Private Collection

547 • Seated Bather, c. 1883-1884
Oil on canvas, 121 x 91 cm
The Fogg Art Museum, Cambridge (Massachusetts)

548 • Suzanne Valadon, 1883-1885
Oil on canvas, 41 x 32 cm
National Gallery of Art, Washington

549 • Lucie Bérard (Girl with White Pinafore), 1884
Oil on canvas, 35 x 27 cm
Private Collection

550 • Madame Renoir in the Garden, 1884
Oil on canvas, 82 x 66 cm
Booth Collection, Detroit

551 • The Summer (Young Woman in a Field of Flowers), 1884
Oil on canvas, 81.2 x 65.7 cm
Private Collection

552 • The Children's Afternoon at Wargemont, 1884
Oil on canvas, 127 x 173 cm
Nationalgalerie, Staatliche Museen, Berlin

553 • The Chrysanthemums, 1884
Oil on canvas, 82 x 66 cm
Musée des Beaux-Arts, Rouen

554 • Still Life, Flowers and Prickly Pears, 1884
Oil on canvas, 74 x 60 cm
Private Collection

555 • View of Argenteuil in Automn, 1884-1885
Oil on canvas, 54 x 65 cm

556 • Still Life. Flowers, 1885
Oil on canvas, 81 x 65 cm
The Solomon R. Guggenheim Museum, New York

557 • Anemones, 1885
Oil on canvas, 31 x 28 cm
The Barnes Foundation, Merion

558 • Girl with Hoop, 1885
Oil on canvas, 125 x 75 cm
National Gallery of Art, Washington

559 • Girl with a Whip, 1885
Oil on canvas, 105 x 75 cm
The Hermitage Museum, St. Petersburg

560 • Bather Arranging Her Hair, 1885
Oil on canvas, 92 x 73 cm
Sterling and Francine Clark Art Institute, Williamstown

545
546
547
548
549
550
551
552
553
554
555
556
557
558
559
560

561

562

563

564

565

566

567

568

569

570

571

572

573

574

575

576

561 • Vase of Flowers, 1885
Oil on canvas, 64 x 53 cm
Private Collection

**562 • Houses at La Roche-Guyon,
c. 1885**
Oil on canvas, 47 x 56 cm
*Aberdeen Art Gallery and Museums,
Aberdeen*

**563 • Aline Charigot (Madame
Renoir), c. 1885**
Oil on canvas, 65 x 54 cm
The Museum of Art, Philadelphia

564 • Gladioli, • 1885
Oil on canvas, 75 x 54.5 cm
Musée d'Orsay, Paris

**565 • Maternity, or Woman
Suckling Her Son, 1886**
Oil on canvas, 81 x 65 cm
Private Collection

566 • Woman with Fan, 1886
Oil on canvas, 56 x 46 cm
The Barnes Foundation, Merion

**567 • Woman Combing Her Blonde
Hair, 1886**
Oil on canvas, 65 x 54 cm
Mc Dermott Collection, New York

**568 • Child at the Breast, or
Maternity, 1886**
Oil on canvas, 74 x 54 cm
*Museum of Fine Arts, Saint Petersburg
(Florida)*

**569 • Return from the Fields,
1886-1887**
Oil on canvas, 53 x 64 cm
Osegawa Collection, Tokyo

**570 • Still Life, Artichokes and
Tomatoes, 1887**
Oil on canvas, 46 x 55 cm
Private Collection

571 • Girls Playing Badminton, 1887
Oil on canvas, 54 x 65 cm
Clark Collection, New York

572 • Bather, 1887
Oil on canvas, 60 x 54 cm
Nasjonalgalleriet, Oslo

**573 • The Bathers
(Grandes baigneuses), 1887**
Oil on canvas, 115 x 170 cm
The Museum of Art, Philadelphia

**574 • Girl with Cat
(Mademoiselle Julie Manet), 1887**
Oil on canvas, 65 x 54 cm
Private Collection

575 • Bather Combing Her Hair, 1887
Oil on canvas, 40 x 31 cm
The National Gallery, London

**576 • Scene in a Brittany Garden,
c. 1887**
Oil on canvas, 54 x 65 cm
The Barnes Foundation, Merion

WORKS

577 • At the Luxembourg Gardens, c. 1887
Oil on canvas, 64 x 53 cm
Private Collection

578 • The Plait, 1884 or 1887
Oil on canvas, 56 x 47 cm
Private Collection

579 • Mediterranean Coast, 1887-1888
Oil on canvas, 25 x 46 cm
Private Collection

580 • Antibes, 1888
Oil on canvas, 65 x 81 cm
A. Hammer Collection, Los Angeles

581 • Catulle Mendès' Daughters at Their Piano, 1888
Oil on canvas, 163 x 130 cm
Annenberg Collection, London

582 • Bougival, 1888
Oil on canvas, 54 x 66 cm
Durand-Ruel Collection, Paris

583 • Seine at Argenteuil, 1888
Oil on canvas, 54 x 65 cm

584 • Seine at Argenteuil, or Le Canot rouge, 1888
Oil on canvas, 54 x 65 cm
The Barnes Foundation, Merion

585 • Child Carrying Flowers, 1888
Oil on canvas, 66 x 54 cm
Museu de Arte, São Paulo

586 • Young Girl with Flower Basket, 1888
Oil on canvas, 80 x 61 cm
Private Collection

587 • Bather, 1888
Oil on canvas, 65 x 54 cm
Private Collection

588 • Woman Bathing Herself, 1888
Oil on canvas, 81 x 65 cm
Kreeger Collection, Washington

589 • The Daughters of Catulle Mendès, 1888
Oil on canvas, 81 x 58 cm
Private Collection

590 • Argenteuil (Sunset), c. 1888
Oil on canvas, 54 x 65 cm
Private Collection

591 • Washerwomen, c. 1888
Oil on canvas, 56 x 47 cm
The Museum of Art, Baltimore

592 • Mont Sainte-Victoire, c. 1888-1889
Oil on canvas, 53 x 64 cm
Yale University Art Gallery, New Haven

577

578

579

580

581

582

583

584

585

586

587

588

589

590

591

592

593

594

595   596   597   598

599   600

601   602   603

604   605   606

607   608

**593 • The Argenteuil Bridge,
c. 1888-1890**
Oil on canvas, 54 x 65 cm
Private Collection

**594 • The Mountain of Sainte-
Victoire, 1889**
Oil on canvas, 55 x 75 cm
The Barnes Foundation, Merion

**595 • Girl with a Basket
of Fish, 1889**
Oil on canvas, 130.7 x 41.8 cm
National Gallery of Art, Washington

**596 • Girl with a Basket
of Oranges, 1889**
Oil on canvas, 130.7 x 41.8 cm
National Gallery of Art, Washington

597 • Flowers and Fruits, 1889
Oil on canvas, 65 x 53 cm
Private Collection

598 • The Piano Lesson, c. 1889
Oil on canvas, 56 x 46 cm
*Joslyn Art Museum, Omaha
(Nebraska)*

**599 • Vases, Basket of Flowers and
Fruits, 1889-1890**
Oil on canvas, 100 x 140 cm
The Museum of Art, Philadelphia

600 • Provençal Landscape, 1890
Oil on canvas, 53.7 x 65.3 cm
*Bayerische
Staatsgemäldesammlungen, Neue
Pinakothek, Munich*

**601 • Large Basket of Summer
Flowers, 1890**
Oil on canvas, 65 x 81 cm
Formerly Cassirer Collection, Berlin

602 • Roses, c. 1890
Oil on canvas, 35.5 x 27 cm
Musée d'Orsay, Paris

603 • In the Meadow, c. 1890
Oil on canvas, 65 x 81 cm
Museum of Fine Arts, Boston

**604 • Picking Flowers
(In the Meadow), c. 1890**
Oil on canvas, 81 x 65 cm
*The Metropolitan Museum of Art,
New York*

605 • Roses in a Vase, c. 1890
Oil on canvas, 29.5 x 33 cm
Musée d'Orsay, Paris

**606 • Still Life with Pomegranates,
1890-1893**
Oil on canvas, 37 x 47 cm
Private Collection

607 • Place de la Trinité, 1890-1895
Oil on canvas, 54 x 65 cm
Niarchos Collection, Paris

608 • Apples on a Plate, 1890-1895
Oil on canvas, 33 x 46 cm

WORKS

609 • The Stroll, 1890-1906
Oil on canvas, 165 x 129 cm
The Barnes Foundation, Merion

610 • View of Essoyes, 1891-1892
Oil on canvas, 32 x 41 cm
Private Collection

611 • Beach at Pornic, 1892
Oil on canvas, 65.5 x 81.5 cm
Private Collection

612 • L'Estaque, 1892
Oil on canvas, 65.5 x 81 cm
Museum of Fine Arts, Boston

613 • Noirmoutier, c. 1892
Oil on canvas, 65 x 81 cm
Oskar Reinhart Foundation,
Winterthur

614 • Young Girls at the piano, 1892
Oil on canvas, 116 x 90 cm
Musée d'Orsay, Paris

615 • The Mouth of the Aven, 1892
Oil on canvas, 46 x 55 cm
Private Collection

616 • Noirmoutier, 1892
Oil on canvas, 65 x 81 cm
The Barnes Foundation, Merion

617 • Bather, 1892
Oil on canvas, 80 x 64 cm
Durand-Ruel Collection, Paris

618 • Bather Seated, 1892
Oil on canvas, 81.5 x 65 cm
The Metropolitan Museum of Art,
New York

619 • Le Square de la Trinité,
c. 1892
Oil on canvas, 53 x 65 cm
Private Collection

620 • The Geese of Pornic, c. 1892
Oil on canvas, 50 x 65 cm
Durand-Ruel Collection, Paris

621 • Bather Arranging Her
Hair, 1893
Oil on canvas, 92 x 74 cm
National Gallery of Art, Washington

622 • Fishing Boats on the Breton
Coast, c. 1893
Oil on canvas, 27 x 46 cm
Private Collection

623 • Village of Essoyes, 1894
Oil on canvas, 54 x 66 cm
Private Collection

624 • Berthe Morisot and Her
Daughter, 1894
Oil on canvas, 81 x 65 cm
Private Collection

609   610
611   612
613   614   615
616   617   618
619   620   621
622   623   624

625

626

627

628

629

630

631

632

633

634

635

636

637

638

639

640

625 • The Reader in Green, c. 1894
Oil on canvas, 26.5 x 21 cm
Musée d'Orsay, Paris

626 • Vase of Flowers, 1895
Oil on canvas, 81 x 54 cm

627 • The Children of Martial Caillebotte, 1895
Oil on canvas, 65 x 82 cm
Private Collection

628 • Gabrielle and Jean, 1895
Oil on canvas, 65 x 54 cm
Musée de l'Orangerie, Paris

629 • The Bay of Douarnenez, c. 1895
Oil on canvas, 54 x 65 cm
Private Collection

630 • Chrysanthemums, c. 1895
Oil on canvas, 32 x 41 cm
Private Collection

631 • Street in Essoyes, 1895-1896
Oil on canvas, 46 x 55 cm

632 • The Spring (Bather Lying Down), 1895-1897
Oil on canvas, 65.4 x 155.6 cm
The Barnes Foundation, Merion

633 • Small Lake with Ducks, c. 1895-1898
Oil on canvas, 54 x 65 cm

634 • Landscape, c. 1895-1900
Oil on canvas, 31 x 40 cm
Private Collection

635 • The Port of la Rochelle, 1896
Oil on canvas, 21 x 32 cm

636 • Port of la Rochelle, 1896
Oil on canvas, 32 x 40 cm
J. Vigeveno Collection, Los Angeles

637 • The Family of the Artist, 1896
Oil on canvas, 173 x 140 cm
The Barnes Foundation, Merion

638 • Bather Standing, 1896
Oil on canvas, 81 x 60 cm
Private Collection

639 • Woman Playing the Guitar, c. 1896-1897
Oil on canvas, 81 x 65 cm
Musée des Beaux-Arts, Lyon

640 • Normandy Landscape, 1897
Oil on canvas, 41 x 56 cm
Private Collection

WORKS

641 • Bathers and Crayfish, 1897
Oil on canvas, 54 x 65 cm
The Museum of Art, Cleveland

642 • Bather Sleeping, 1897
Oil on canvas, 81 x 65 cm
Kunstmuseum, Winterthur

**643 • Yvonne and Christine Lerolle
at the Piano, 1897**
Oil on canvas, 73 x 92 cm
Musée de l'Orangerie, Paris

644 • Jean Renoir with a Hoop, 1898
Oil on canvas, 66 x 50 cm
Private Collection

645 • Lunch at Berneval, 1898
Oil on canvas, 82 x 66 cm
Private Collection

646 • Anemones, c. 1898
Oil on canvas, 58 x 49 cm
Rosenberg Collection, New York

**647 • Gabrielle Arising
(The Awakening), 1899**
Oil on canvas, 63 x 53 cm
The Barnes Foundation, Merion

648 • Self-Portrait, 1899 (?)
Oil on canvas, 41 x 33 cm
*Sterling and Francine Clark Art
Institute, Williamstown*

649 • Landscape at Beaulieu, c. 1900
Oil on canvas, 65 x 81 cm
Private Collection

650 • Road to Essoyes, 1901
Oil on canvas, 46.2 x 55.2 cm
Private Collection

**651 • Madame Gaston Bernheim de
Villers, 1901**
Oil on canvas, 93 x 73 cm
Musée d'Orsay, Paris

**652 • Pheasant and Other
Fowl, 1902**
Oil on canvas, 54 x 65 cm
Private Collection

653 • White Pierrot, c. 1902
Oil on canvas, 81 x 62 cm
The Institute of Arts, Detroit

654 • Bather Drying Herself, c. 1902
Oil on canvas, 100 x 73 cm
The Barnes Foundation, Merion

655 • Houses at Cannet, c. 1902
Oil on canvas, 39 x 54 cm
The Barnes Foundation, Merion

641   642   643

644   645   646   647

648   649

650   651   652

653

654   655

656

657

658

659

660

661

662

663

664

665

666

667

668

669

670

656 • Bather, c. 1903
Oil on canvas, 92 x 73 cm
Kunsthistorisches Museum, Vienna

657 • Ode to the Flowers
(According to Anacreon), 1903-1909
Oil on canvas, 46 x 36 cm
Musée d'Orsay, Paris

658 • Claude Renoir in Arabian
Dress, 1904
Oil on canvas, 55 x 48 cm
The Barnes Foundation, Merion

659 • Versailles, c. 1904
Oil on canvas, 63 x 52 cm
Robert Lehman Foundation, New York

660 • The Baby's Breakfast, c. 1904
Oil on canvas, 65 x 54 cm
Private Collection

661 • The Baker, c. 1904
Oil on canvas, 65 x 54 cm
Niarchos Collection, Paris

662 • The Needlewomen, 1904-1905
Oil on canvas, 100 x 81 cm
The Barnes Foundation, Merion

663 • Portrait of Coco, 1905
Oil on canvas, 35 x 30 cm
Private Collection

664 • Woman in Oriental
Dress, 1905
Oil on canvas, 81 x 65 cm
Private Collection

665 • Landscape at Cagnes, 1905
Oil on canvas, 46 x 55 cm
Private Collection

666 • Terrace in Cagnes, 1905
Oil on canvas, 46 x 55.5 cm
Bridgestone Museum of Art, Tokyo

667 • Strawberries, c. 1905
Oil on canvas, 28 x 46 cm
Musée de l'Orangerie, Paris

668 • Coco's Writing Lesson,
1906-1907
Oil on canvas, 54 x 65 cm
The Barnes Foundation, Merion

669 • Reclining Nude, 1906-1907
Oil on canvas, 67 x 160 cm
Musée de l'Orangerie, Paris

670 • White Roses, 1907
Oil on canvas, 26 x 30 cm

128

WORKS

671 • Landscape Seen from the House of Cagnes, 1907
Oil on canvas, 32.5 x 46 cm
Private Collection

672 • Gabrielle with Open Blouse, 1907
Oil on canvas, 66.5 x 53.5 cm
Durand-Ruel Collection, Paris

673 • Woman with Fan, 1908
Oil on canvas, 65 x 54 cm
Private Collection

674 • Portrait of Ambroise Vollard, 1908
Oil on canvas, 81 x 64 cm
Courtauld Institute Galleries, London

675 • Medlar Trees, 1908
Oil on canvas, 25 x 43 cm
Private Collection

676 • Landscape Around Nice, 1908
Oil on canvas, 45 x 59 cm
Private Collection

677 • Strawberries, 1908
Oil on canvas, 23 x 39 cm
Private Collection

678 • Judgment of Paris, 1908
Oil on canvas, 81 x 100 cm
Private Collection

679 • Young Girl with Straw Hat, c. 1908
Oil on canvas, 46 x 35 cm
Musée d'Orsay, Paris

680 • Bather Injured, 1909
Oil on canvas, 92 x 73 cm
Private Collection

681 • Dancer with Tambourine, 1909
Oil on canvas, 155 x 65 cm
The National Gallery, London

682 • Dancer with Castanets, 1909
Oil on canvas, 155 x 65 cm
The National Gallery, London

683 • Nude Lying Down from the Back, or The Bather Resting , 1909
Oil on canvas, 41 x 52 cm
Musée d'Orsay, Paris

684 • The Clown, 1909
Oil on canvas, 120 x 77 cm
Musée de l'Orangerie, Paris

685 • Bust of Nude Woman, 1909
Oil on canvas, 48 x 56 cm
The Barnes Foundation, Merion

671 672 673 674 675 676 677 678 679 680 681 682 683 684 685

686

687

688

689   690

691

692   693

694   695

696   697

698

699   700

686 • Roses in a Decorated Vase, 1909
Oil on canvas, 55 x 46 cm

687 • Young Girl Seated, c. 1909
Oil on canvas, 65.5 x 54.5 cm
Musée d'Orsay, Paris

688 • Caryatids, 1910
Oil on canvas, 130 x 45 cm
The Barnes Foundation, Merion

689 • Caryatids, 1910
Oil on canvas, 130 x 45 cm
The Barnes Foundation, Merion

690 • Reclining Nude, 1910
Oil on canvas, 67.3 x 154.9 cm
The Barnes Foundation, Merion

691 • Self-Portrait with White Hat, 1910
Oil on canvas, 42 x 33 cm
Private Collection

692 • After Bathing, 1910
Oil on canvas, 95 x 76 cm
The Barnes Foundation, Merion

693 • Portrait of Paul Durand-Ruel, 1910
Oil on canvas, 65 x 54 cm
Durand-Ruel Collection, Paris

694 • Self-Portrait, 1910
Oil on canvas, 47 x 36 cm
Private Collection

695 • Portrait of Madame Renoir, 1910
Oil on canvas, 81 x 65 cm
Wadsworth Atheneum, Hartford

696 • Monsieur and Madame Bernheim de Villers, 1910
Oil on canvas, 81 x 65.5 cm
Musée d'Orsay, Paris

697 • Landscape at Cannes, c. 1910
Oil on canvas, 54 x 65 cm
Private Collection

698 • The Toilet: Woman Combing Her Hair, before 1910
Oil on canvas, 55 x 46.5 cm
Musée d'Orsay, Paris

699 • Gabrielle with Jewelry, c. 1910
Oil on canvas, 82 x 66 cm
Private Collection

700 • Bather Drying Her Leg, c. 1910-1911
Oil on canvas, 84 x 65 cm
Museu de Arte, São Paulo

**701 • Gabrielle Before the Mirror,
c. 1910-1913**
Oil on canvas, 81 x 65 cm
Bernheim-Jeune Collection, Paris

**702 • The Rhône and the Saône,
1910-1915**
Oil on canvas, 92 x 74 cm
Private Collection

**703 • Bather in the Forest,
c. 1910-1915**
Oil on canvas, 92 x 73 cm
Bührle Collection, Zurich

704 • Gabrielle with Rose, 1911
Oil on canvas, 55 x 47 cm
Musée d'Orsay, Paris

**705 • Madame Joseph
Durand-Ruel, 1911**
Oil on canvas, 92 x 73 cm
Durand-Ruel Collection, Paris

**706 • The Young Alexandre
Thurneyssen Dressed as
a Shepherd, 1911**
Oil on canvas, 75 x 93 cm
*Museum of Art, Rhode Island School
of Design, Providence*

**707 • Meeting in the Garden,
c. 1911-1915**
Oil on canvas, 55 x 65 cm
Musée d'Orsay, Paris

**708 • Madame de Galéa on the
Deckchair, 1912**
Oil on canvas, 114 x 162 cm
Private Collection

**709 • Still Life : Cup, Lemon,
Coffee Pot, c. 1912**
Oil on canvas, 55 x 65 cm
Musée d'Orsay, Paris

710 • The Laundress, c. 1912
Oil on canvas, 92 x 73 cm
Private Collection

711 • The Laundress, c. 1912
Oil on canvas, 65 x 55 cm
*The Metropolitan Museum of Art,
New York*

**712 • Young Woman with Rose, also
called Woman in Blue, 1913**
Oil on canvas, 65.5 x 54.5 cm
Musée d'Orsay, Paris

**713 • Judgment of Paris,
c. 1913-1914**
Oil on canvas, 73 x 91 cm
Musée d'Art, Hiroshima

714 • The Collettes, 1914
Oil on canvas, 54 x 65 cm
*The Metropolitan Museum of Art,
New York*

715 • Portrait of Tilla Durieux, 1914
Oil on canvas, 92 x 74 cm
*The Metropolitan Museum of Art,
New York*

701

702

703

704

705

706

707

708

709

710

711

712

713

714

715

716

717

718

719

720

721

722

723

724

725

726

727

728

729

716 • Reader Dressed in White, 1915-1916
Oil on canvas, 21.5 x 20.5 cm
Musée d'Orsay, Paris

717 • Sleeping Odalisque (Odalisque with Slippers), c. 1915-1917
Oil on canvas, 50 x 53 cm
Musée d'Orsay, Paris

718 • Landscape at Antibes, c. 1915-1917
Oil on canvas, 27 x 40 cm
The Barnes Foundation, Merion

719 • Odalisque, c. 1915-1917
Oil on canvas, 46 x 36 cm
The Barnes Foundation, Merion

720 • Roses, 1915-1917
Oil on canvas, 28 x 30 cm
Private Collection

721 • Madeleine Bruno (Two Bathers), 1916
Oil on canvas, 92 x 73 cm
Private Collection

722 • Bathers, 1916
Oil on canvas, 67 x 92 cm
The Barnes Foundation, Merion

723 • Ambroise Vollard in Bullfighter's Costume, 1917
Oil on canvas, 103 x 83 cm
Nippon Television Network Corporation, Tokyo

724 • Woman Resting, 1917-1919
Oil on canvas, 23 x 32 cm
Musée de l'Orangerie, Paris

725 • Fruit Basket with Apples, Grapes, and Green Figs, 1918
Oil on canvas, 26 x 34 cm
Private Collection

726 • Bathers, c. 1918
Oil on canvas, 80 x 65 cm
The Barnes Foundation, Merion

727 • Bathers, c. 1918-1919
Oil on canvas, 110 x 160 cm
Musée d'Orsay, Paris

728 • Woman with Mandolin, 1919
Oil on canvas, 55 x 55 cm
Alex Hillman Foundation, New York

729 • The Concert, c. 1919
Oil on canvas, 75.6 x 92.7 cm
Art Gallery of Ontario, Toronto

Bibliography

J. Baudot, *Renoir, ses amis, ses modèles,* Paris, 1949

F. Daulte, *Auguste Renoir, catalogue raisonné de l'œuvre peint,* Lausanne, 1971

A. Distel, *Renoir, "Il faut embellir",* (Découvertes Gallimard), Paris, 1993

E. Fezzi, *Tout l'œuvre peint de Renoir. Période impressionniste 1869-1883,* Paris, 1985

Ch.S. Moffet, *The New Painting. Impressionism 1874-1876,* catalogue of the Exhibition, Fine Arts Museum of San Francisco; National Gallery of Art, Washington, 1986

S. Monneret, *Renoir,* Paris, 1989

S. Monneret, *Dictionnaire de l'Impressionnisme et son époque,* Paris, 1978 ("Collection Bouquins", 1987)

Renoir, catalogue of the Exhibition, Hayward Gallery, London; Galeries nationales du Grand Palais, Paris; Museum of Fine Arts, Boston, 1985-1986

J. Renoir, *Renoir, my Father,* London, 1962

J. Rewald, *The History of Impressionism,* 4th ed., New York, 1973

N. Wadley, *Renoir : A Retrospective,* New York, 1989

B.E. White, *Renoir,* New York, 1984